HEART OF THE MATTER

How to Conquer Stress Before It Wreaks
Havoc on Your Body, Mind and Soul

HEART OF THE MATTER

How to Conquer Stress Before It Wreaks
Havoc on Your Body, Mind and Soul

By Dr. Barry Dinner, MBBCH, ABAARM

First Edition 2020

ISBN: 978-1-7328884-3-2

Library of Congress Control Number: 2020903230

LCCN Imprint Name: Beyoung Health INC

Printed in the United States of America

Published by Beyoung Health INC
Baltimore, Maryland

Visit: beyoung.life
Email: info@beyoung.life

AUTHOR'S CONTACT INFORMATION

Dr. Barry Dinner, MBBCH, ABAARM

Beyoung Health Inc
410-943-7085
info@beyoung.life

Stay informed about the latest Anti-Aging developments, supplements and products. Subscribe to Dr. Barry Dinner's monthly newsletter, that provides practical advice on how you can truly "add life to your years" as well as "years to your life".

Go to www.beyoung.life and subscribe now!

DISCLAIMER

The materials and content contained in this book are for general information and educational purposes only and are not intended to be a substitute for professional medical advice, diagnosis or treatment. None of the information in this book should ever be interpreted as a claim of treatment or cure of any medical condition.

Readers of this book should not rely exclusively on information provided in this book for their own health needs. All specific medical questions should be presented to your own health care provider. Diagnosis and treatment of any medical conditions are strictly for you to discuss with your doctor.

The intention of this book is to provide information about anti-aging. We also have attempted to provide anti-aging guidelines for maintaining your youth. None of the information in this book, and none of the guidelines, should ever be interpreted as claims of diagnosis, treatment, or cure of any medical condition.

Beyoung Health Inc and Dr. Barry Dinner do not assume any risk for your use of this book. In consideration for your use of this book, you agree that in no event will Beyoung Health Inc and Dr. Barry Dinner be liable to you in any manner whatsoever for any decision made or action or non-action taken by you in reliance upon the information provided through this book.

TABLE OF CONTENTS

ABOUT THE AUTHOR

Dr. Barry Dinner is a highly respected anti-aging physician, whose integrative approach to life extension has enabled him to imbue a healthy and meaningful quality of life into all those who seek his counsel. Dr. Dinner's anti-aging LIFE Protocol is predicated on three pillars — Lifespan, Youthspan and Valuespan — that have rekindled the youth of patients around the world.

Having graduated from the highly esteemed South African University of Witwatersrand's (WITS) Medical School with a bachelor's degree of Medicine and Surgery, Dr. Dinner's career spans more than thirty-three years, in that he developed sophisticated and advanced pro-active programs for preventive medicine in family practices, as well as serving as medical director for a 500-bed geriatrics hospital. Moreover, Dr. Dinner founded the highly successful Corporate Stress Institute of SA, having partnered with acclaimed psychology professors at the WITS School of Business in order to devise a program that combined both stress and health management.

After having practiced a wide range of medical disciplines, such as internal medicine, psychiatry, pediatrics, dermatology, obstetrics and gynecology, Dr. Dinner completed his fellowship in anti-aging and regenerative medicine with the American Academy of Anti-Aging Medicine in 2010.

Today, Dr. Dinner is active as an anti-aging practitioner and is the author of *Be Young*. He is the founder of Ignite Your Youth anti-aging nutritional supplements, an out-branch of his anti-aging clinic for advanced testing, cardiovascular health, brain health, bioidentical hormone replacement therapy, the management of metabolic illnesses, nutritional and fitness programs, as well as stress and adrenal fatigue management.

ACKNOWLEDGMENTS

I have written this book based on my life's experience together with many years of working in the trenches as a family physician. I therefore owe my gratitude to the countless patients and colleagues who have provided me with a mosaic of fascinating and often heartwarming relationships — people from all walks of life striving to be well and to make the most of their lives.

I must acknowledge my brilliant teachers, especially in the functional medicine and anti-aging field, who expanded the horizons of medicine and healing for me.

I would like to thank my friends who, over the years, have taught me the meaning of a purposeful relationship.

I would like to thank Naomi Chait for her countless hours and fine expertise in bringing this book to fruition.

I have an endless amount of gratitude to my amazing wife and children for their ongoing love and support.

FOREWORD

When reading Dr. Barry Dinner's book on managing stress, readers will appreciate the warm laid-back style. But beneath the ease, there is a bit of steel. Dr. Dinner expects change! He expects his patients to transform their old approaches to stress. He expects greater well-being.

His purpose is compelling. Evidence for the damage of stress is irrefutable. However, when overwhelmed by stress people often feel defeated. This manual helps us see past helplessness and toward healing and recovery. If we can change stressful situations, we must. If we cannot, we must accept them but must work to alter our take on them. It helps to see the stressor at a distance, outside of us; inside we are whole. Unharmed, we can advocate for ourselves in the best way possible.

Developing resilience toward stress is a great gift. It can spell the difference between the downward spiral of disease and the upward spiral toward health and recovery.

This small book is a gem. It compresses a great deal of information and wisdom into a slim volume. It is written with — I daresay — love. Here is your own gifted healer; your own devoted Dr. Dinner challenging you to change, to do better. He believes in you. There is a great power in support.

He is with you. He is waiting for your success.

Dr. Judy Belsky, PhD

Clinical Psychologist

Specialist in Trauma and Stress Recovery

PART I

CONQUERING STRESS

INTRODUCTION

There has been amazing medical progress in preventing many serious illnesses. Obviously identifying the causes that result in disease is essential in order to successfully prevent them, and physicians are screening for many risk factors. However, one area is being overlooked by many and is in fact a major cause for numerous medical problems. This factor is STRESS, and because it has such a profound effect on health, it must be detected and treated.

Stress can lead to illness in people who otherwise maintain a healthy lifestyle. Heart attack, stroke and many types of cancers, as well as cognitive impairment and dementia are all linked to chronic stress. The medical data shows a strong connection between these illnesses and stress, but because it is difficult to measure, I believe the correlation is much greater than is being formally recognized. From an anecdotal point of view, I have seen a distinct link between stress and many cancer patients, although the causal connection with stress and heart attack is much more obvious.

It is not uncommon to find a patient who lives a healthy lifestyle, has good blood parameters and appears to be a low risk candidate for suffering from a serious illness, yet he ends up in the emergency room with a stroke or heart attack.

Introduction

A patient in his mid-60s came to my office recently complaining of chest pain. He held a very stressful job as a dentist and spent most of his day pleasing patients, dealing with children who would not cooperate and trying to stay on time with a busy waiting room filled with patients. He decided to begin exercising to get into shape and start taking care of himself. That is when the chest pain began. A cardiogram came back normal, his cholesterol was normal, and his blood tests were all fine. However, the stress test was abnormal, and an angiogram picked up a blockage of his coronary arteries. Stress was likely a major factor contributing to his coronary heart disease.

It is therefore imperative that we gain a full understanding of stress, its impact on our health and how to manage it effectively in order to optimize our well-being and ensure longevity.

This book is designed to help you understand the meaning of stress, the role it plays in our daily lives and to provide a real solution to achieving a relatively stress-free lifestyle. The **7C system,** which makes up the core of this book, is a unique way of determining the **source** of your stress and finding the **solution** to managing it. Essentially, stress occurs when we feel we do not have control of a situation, and as long as we remain in this state, the stress will linger. We need to acquire tools to help us recognize the root of our problem and to regain control. This is the essence of this book.

ooo

THE BODY IS COMPRISED OF TWO NERVOUS SYSTEMS, THE SYMPATHETIC AND THE PARASYMPATHETIC SYSTEMS. Both systems have networks of nerves running from the brain and spinal cord that supply nerves to all the main organs of the body, including the vascular system.

The sympathetic and parasympathetic nervous systems can be compared to a generator supplying electricity to a household. One set of circuits provides cooling to all parts of the house, and the other provides circuits to heat up the house. They cannot blow hot and cold at the same time; it is either one or the other.

Fight or Flight

The sympathetic chain of nerves is "switched on" or activated when there is a need for the fight-or-flight reaction that occurs when we perceive danger. Initially, the response begins with the hypothalamus, which is an area in the brain that sends a message to the inner part of the adrenal gland called the adrenal medulla (this gland sits on top of the kidneys). When the adrenal medulla is stimulated, it releases a hormone called adrenaline or epinephrine, which increases blood pressure and pulse rate, widens the small airways in the lungs, dilates the pupils and sharpens sight and hearing in order to help us deal with the danger.

As the initial surge of adrenaline subsides, the hypothalamus in the brain activates the second component of the stress response, called the HPA axis. This consists of the hypothalamus in the brain, the pituitary gland at the base of the brain and the adrenal cortex, which is the outer part of the adrenal gland that rests above the kidneys. The adrenal cortex releases a hormone called cortisol, that in turn results in a number of reactions in the body, including increased blood pressure and the release of glucose from storage organs into the blood vessels. When you experience chronic stress, this system is turned on with full force and is associated with many of the health problems caused by stress.

Rest and Digest

The parasympathetic nervous system is connected to the organ systems by way of the vagus nerve. The influence of this nerve and how it affects us is called "vagal tone." It is responsible for the release of the neurotransmitter called acetylcholine, that helps restore the body to a state of calm and balance and allows it to relax and repair. The parasympathetic nervous system, which is often referred to as the rest-and-digest system, maintains the body systems and enables the GI tract, the heart and many other essential organs to function efficiently. Not only is it optimal to maintain a strong vagal tone (this will be discussed in more detail further on), but it is also imperative that we strive to live most of our lives in parasympathetic mode and to resolve to turn off the sympathetic nervous system, which should only be used to escape acute danger.

There are many books describing relaxation techniques and methods on how to turn off the sympathetic overdrive and stop the stress response. These are all useful techniques that help, but they do not address the essential origin and the method of treating the root causes of stress. Therefore, the main objective of this book is to discuss the mechanism and basic concepts that will enable you to live your life in a more relaxed manner and remain in parasympathetic mode.

You should not view this book as providing techniques to fend off stress, but rather as advice on how to maintain a relatively stress-free life. It is advisable to review this book again after completing it to help you transform your lifestyle and shift into a more relaxed and constructive mode.

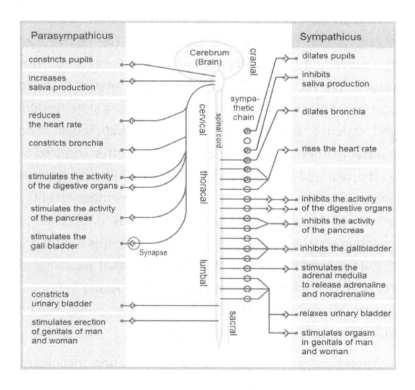

Parasympathicus		Sympathicus
constricts pupils	Cerebrum (Brain)	dilates pupils
increases saliva production		inhibits saliva production
reduces the heart rate	sympa-thetic chain	dilates bronchia
constricts bronchia		rises the heart rate
stimulates the activity of the digestive organs		
stimulates the activity of the pancreas		inhibits the acitivity of the digestive organs
stimulates the gall bladder	Synapse	inhibits the activity of the pancreas
		inhibits the gallbladder
		stimulates the adrenal medulla to release adrenaline and noradrenaline
constricts urinary bladder		
stimulates erection of genitals of man and woman		relaxes urinary bladder
		stimulates orgasm in genitals of man and woman

cranial · cervical · spinal cord · thoracal · lumbal · sacral

CHAPTER 1

The Danger of Living in Sympathetic Mode

The sympathetic nervous system is stimulated by the fight-or-flight mode. When your brain perceives danger or the need to switch into the fight-or-flight response, it triggers the sympathetic nervous system.

This first perception may be due to a legitimate threat, such as an aggressor in the form of a human or animal, or a real physical danger. An example of this would be how you would feel flying through tremendous turbulence or experiencing the ground shaking during an earthquake. Your body would react in the following way; your heart rate would increase, your pupils would dilate, and your hands would become cold and sweaty. When the stress stimulus continues, then cortisol is produced by the adrenal cortex in order to maintain your vigilance and ability to cope with a threatening situation.

This response can also occur when your brain perceives something as a threat. The threat may present itself in the form of a person whose presence unsettles you, an upcoming speech you are required to give, an approaching deadline, or the like. The brain will not distinguish perceived threats such as these from real physical threats, and the same nervous reactions will be set off.

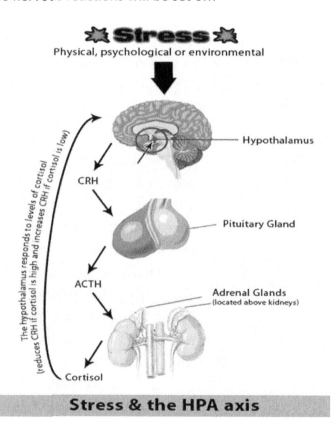

Stress & the HPA axis

The Danger of Living in Sympathetic Mode

These stress hormones that are released and circulated to the different organs in the body are required purely for an acute reaction (short term) to help you overcome any immediate danger. The problem occurs when these hormones remain at high levels in your system due to ongoing stress, resulting in a TOXIC effect. The rhythm of the heart is affected, and the normal Heart Rate Variability (HRV) that is healthy for you will be disturbed. As a result, the chance of developing dangerous arrhythmias (an irregular heart rhythm) is greatly increased.

Additional repercussions of chronic stress are that the blood vessels to essential organs become constricted, and blood flow is shifted away from the kidneys and bowels where it is needed for normal digestion and waste elimination. Many metabolic changes also occur, including increased glucose in the blood and an elevated risk of developing diabetes, as well as an escalation in the production of lipids, which are unhealthy fats in the blood. High cortisol ensues, and this can also contribute to weight gain.

The bottom line is that the effects of chronic stress can override any positive effects that other good habits may be providing, and your health—which may be generally good—can be severely compromised merely because you are stressed.

CHAPTER 2

The Benefits of Remaining in Parasympathetic Mode

It is a top priority to remain relatively stress-free in your life and to switch off the stress response that was described above. Even if you are exposed to some sort of stress, make sure it does not affect you to the extent that it can have an influence on your health.

The body's overall ability to function well is notably influenced by your stress levels. Particular attention should be focused on avoiding stressful situations, in order to evade the constant battering caused by high adrenaline and cortisol. Even accelerated aging of the brain can be attributed to stress.

Therefore, living in a constant carefree and relaxed mode may be one of the major determinants of physical and mental wellness and long life. This style of living will ensure that the sympathetic nervous system is "switched off" and the parasympathetic nervous system is active. It is imperative that you put some real time and effort into staying in parasympathetic mode most of the time. Weight loss is almost impossible if you are not in a relaxed mode, and the benefits to heart health, to vascular health, and to good digestion can be attributed to remaining stress-free. The benefits to brain health and all your metabolic processes, including preventing diabetes, are also well documented.

I have mentioned above how the vagus nerve connects and influences the body systems. This includes the immune system, which plays a central role in causing many disease processes, such as multiple sclerosis, Crohn's disease, colitis, autoimmune thyroid disease and Alzheimer's disease, amongst other syndromes. Although elevated stress levels are associated with increased autoimmune diseases, the converse is also true, in that high vagal tone can decrease autoimmune diseases.

The vagus nerve provides the many benefits of the parasympathetic nervous system. It has now been discovered that chemicals that initiate inflammation and autoimmune problems can be suppressed by the vagus nerve. It has also been found that people who have low vagal tone and have a heart attack are prone to getting lethal arrhythmias (irregular rhythm of the heart). Therefore, increasing the influence of the vagus nerve most of the time is critical to our overall health.

Heart of the Matter

CHAPTER 3

Recognizing That You Are in Stress Mode

You may sometimes feel the obvious symptoms of stress and can take steps to avoid it, but frequently people become used to the stress status and fail to recognize it. Stress becomes a so-called "normal" state, and we believe that life with stress is inevitable and part of our everyday routine. For you to take action to reduce it, it is essential to recognize that you are in a stressed mode and that it is not natural to continue like this.

Unfortunately, living in the 21st century is extremely demanding, even though it is a generation of time-saving technological advancements. Long working hours, difficulty paying off debts, a need for instant responses and being connected all the time, and an increase in violence worldwide are just some of the factors that contribute to a more stressful lifestyle.

The message here is: Be aware of stress; don't ignore it. Do not accept a reality where stress is part of the job and because you are so used to it, you can handle the effects. This is not the case, and you need to deal with the situation in the same way as you would if you needed to quit smoking or break another bad habit.

It is important to know that there are many factors that activate the stress response, causing the stress hormones to be secreted in excess. Two common conditions related to out-of-control stress and the severe consequences of a chronic stress response are (a) adrenal fatigue and burnout and (b) anxiety.

(a) Adrenal Fatigue and Burnout

Stress initially manifests itself with an increase in cortisol levels in your body, causing you to become wired and to overreact to simple stressors. If it is not addressed timeously, you will remain in this state and have the symptoms and complications of high cortisol. Since high cortisol levels are not good for the brain, eventually the brain institutes a feedback mechanism to suppress cortisol production in the adrenal gland. This is the second stage of adrenal fatigue, when cortisol levels plummet. The low cortisol levels leave you feeling flat, exhausted and unable to cope with the daily demands of life. This is called adrenal fatigue or burnout.

Here is a typical example. I have a 30-year-old female patient who has 3 children, works most of the day and is simultaneously completing a master's degree in psychology. After work, she comes home to constant demands from her children, housework and the nighttime bed routine, as well as the pressure of completing papers for her degree. There is no down time and little chance of recovering. She is functioning with constant chronic stress and depleted levels of cortisol. This has manifest itself in extreme fatigue and feeling overwhelmed by life.

(b) Anxiety

Anxiety is a common phenomenon that we all experience to a greater or lesser extent. A real danger will obviously arouse feelings of anxiety, but there are many people who feel anxious because they perceive danger — even if it is not real. This perceived danger or threat may cause as much anxiety as a very real danger, and the stress response will be of the same magnitude in both situations.

For example, the anxiety of a person who believes they have a life-threatening illness, even though it is not true, will be as great as a soldier who is facing a life-threatening situation in combat. Both perceive that their life is being threatened.

Undoubtedly, there is always an underlying cause for anxiety, whether it is real or perceived, but it is often hidden in the subconscious and not recognized at all. The trigger may occur due to an impending meeting or exam, an underlying fear that originated in your past, or any other phobia or challenge that emanated when you were younger and was previously buried in the back of your mind. Although you may never actively think about this fear, the anxiety may show itself when it is triggered by a thought, feeling or other stimulus that suddenly rejuvenates the forgotten angst. This anxiety, if it occurs frequently, takes its toll on your stress response.

I have a patient, a generally healthy 63-year-old male, who out of the blue did not feel well, and he checked his blood pressure. It was moderately high, and he came into my office in quite a panic. I did a full work-up on him and prescribed medication to control his blood pressure. However, from then on, every time he didn't feel well, he would check his blood pressure and if it was slightly elevated, he would rush to the emergency room in panic mode — that pushed his blood pressure even higher. He perceived his elevated blood pressure as a real danger to him and cause for alarm. This is an example of acute anxiety triggering the stress response.

Stress related to illness is a very common source of anxiety but is only one of many causes. Again, it is important to identify where the anxiety originates from and to treat the root cause in order to slow down the stress response.

I have mentioned how critical it is to recognize that you are stressed. Below is a list of symptoms that occur as a result of being stressed. If you experience one or more of them, you should be alerted to check your health further.

CHAPTER 4

Symptoms of Sympathetic Overdrive

- Waking in the morning and experiencing an anxious feeling usually in the chest and the upper abdomen
- Cold and often sweaty hands
- Rapid pulse even when not exercising
- Chest pain and heart palpitations
- Rapid breathing and feeling the need to breathe deeply; feeling that you cannot get enough air
- Tight muscles, especially in the neck and back
- Frequent muscle twitches in the face and around the eyes
- Abdominal pains, diarrhea or irritable bowel syndrome
- Frequent headaches, especially coming from the neck
- Lightheadedness, faintness and dizziness
- Feeling moody and irritable or depressed
- Feeling overloaded or overwhelmed
- Dry mouth and difficulty swallowing
- Clenched jaw and grinding teeth

Symptoms of Sympathetic Overdrive

- Frequent colds, infections and cold sores
- Weight gain or loss without dieting
- Insomnia, sleep disturbances or bad dreams
- Poor productivity and reliability at work and in general
- Difficulty making decisions

Please note that there may be other causes for the above symptoms, and it is advisable that you consult with your health practitioner if you experience any number of these symptoms.

The first step then is to recognize that you are experiencing stress. Following this, you need to focus on managing it as seriously as you would manage any other significant health risk or poor health habit.

A Daily Log can help you learn about your own stress responses.

STRESSOR	YOUR RESPONSE	RATE IT 1-10
What initiated the response	*How did you feel during the stress response?*	*Get to know what produces high stress in you.*
Example: Argument with spouse over priorities of spending money	*Mentally:* Confused as to how to react *Emotionally:* Angry at unfair approach *Physically (Where in your body did you experience it?)* Tight chest and neck muscles	*Differing ideas and perceptions as to how to spend monthly income*

2	Mentally: Emotionally: Physically (Where in your body did you experience it?)	

CHAPTER 5

Methods for Staying in Parasympathetic Drive

Once you have recognized that you are under stress, you must identify the root cause in order to find a solution. To this end, I will now discuss ways of recognizing the real causes of stress and sympathetic overdrive, and in so doing, put into place various approaches to help break away from this unhealthy mode. The following seven areas—the 7 Cs— cover many of the core issues leading to stress. There are of course other less common problems, but covering these seven will enable you to pinpoint a possible originator that can jumpstart the healing process. It is important to become familiar with these 7C principles to help you tackle and treat stress, and to give you tools to eradicate it.

Once the stressors have been removed, you need to shift into a relaxed, productive and creative mode. There are activities that make you feel good and at peace and allow vagal tone to predominate. They are described in Part II of this book and include being creative, contributing time or energy to others, improving yourself or doing your job thoroughly and with completion. They are all "feel good" activities that literally give you a warm feeling in your chest. This is vagal tone.

Then there are social activities. Close or even familiar social contacts have been proven to increase vagal tone. When you walk around your neighborhood and people know you and greet you, and you have people to talk to and friendly neighbors that you can borrow things from when needed, it contributes to vagal tone. Work on developing worthwhile relationships and keeping in touch with friends and family.

Finally, there are techniques. They are described below and are known to switch on the vagus, parasympathetic system. These are short techniques that should be applied or used during the day. They will help the vagal tone predominate and thereby set into motion many of the healthy processes that are modulated by the vagus nerve.

•

The 7C Core Program to Reduce Stress

5.1   Control

A stressful state can result from not being in control of a situation. A classic example is when your health is compromised. You experience the feeling of something going wrong and not being able to do anything about it. This is extremely stressful. The waiting period to receive a medical diagnosis is much more nerve-wracking than finally getting a result and formulating a plan of action to treat the sickness and begin the recovery process. This is obviously due to the feeling of absolute helplessness before being provided with a treatment plan. You feel like a victim with no control over your situation, which is both frightening and extremely trying.

Financial stresses, work conditions and toxic interpersonal relationships are other examples of circumstances that may be beyond your control. Financial hardships can force you to remain in an unhealthy work environment because you are dependent on your income for financial stability. This makes you dread going to work — but at the same time you are unable to resign for fear of not being able to find an alternative source of income. This leaves you stuck between needing your salary but despising your stressful work environment. You are helpless and not in control of the situation.

When your finances are in a mess, you feel helpless and cannot see any way to gain control over it. This is an extremely common phenomenon, and those of you who have experienced financial difficulties are aware of how stressed and incapable they make you feel.

Ongoing debt and the inability to make ends meet often results in taking additional loans in order to cover everyday expenses and pay the bills. In these cases, even small monetary needs, such as money for your children's school trips, can seem overwhelming. You may make use of more than one credit card, hoping that by the time the due dates approach, more money will come in. However, your income is limited, and when the bills fall due, you are extremely stressed and feel out of control.

A toxic marriage, where there are financial obligations and children involved, can leave you paralyzed, with no escape from the tension. You would like to walk out of the marriage, but the ramifications are too serious — you feel trapped.

Now, it is no use telling you to just walk away from these different situations, because you ARE trapped. It is important that you devise a plan of action to overcome or resolve the problematic situation, because the feeling of being trapped is not going to go away or improve without taking action.

So how do you overcome these situations?

Firstly, recognize that you have lost control and pinpoint the area in which it is occurring. This may be an obvious step, but we frequently choose not to deal with a problem and prefer to leave it on the "back burner," hoping that the problem will resolve itself. We ignore the consequences of this severe stress because we cannot face dealing with it. This is the same as if you ignore a mechanical problem with your car; it will not fix itself but rather eventually break altogether. So too, you need to take the essential step of pinpointing your issue and resolving to deal with it.

Secondly, you need to strategize how to take control. Make this a priority, and look at all the resources that you can use in order to achieve this. It is important to take time to analyze the situation and look at all possible solutions. Speak to experienced people who can help you formulate a plan.

Thirdly, if necessary, you may have to make a brave decision; you may have to be a hero. You may have to risk leaving your job and going out on your own. Or you may have to change your attitude in your marriage — even if you think you are right and your spouse is the one who should make the changes. You may have to make some fundamental financial decisions to take control of your finances, such as living on a budget or doing some additional work to bring in the extra money that is needed.

In other words, you need to take some sort of action to start the process of rectifying the problem. It is helpful to try and implement some support systems to fall back on and, from time to time, stop and reassess the situation, check your progress and make any necessary adjustments to your plan of action.

We want to change our routine and eliminate unhealthy responses to stress that compromise our well-being. One way to adopt change is via the acronym A-C-E.

A = Accept

C = Change

E = Eliminate

Let's begin with **A** for Accept. What can you _not_ change? Examples are the death of loved ones or enduring illness in people close to us.

If you try too hard to change what you cannot change, you will be stressed indeed. You need to use all your maturity to truly accept what must be endured and to avoid adding insult to injury by fighting too hard against the inevitable. Joining support groups, where you give and receive support, can go a long way to truly learning to **accept**.

Next, you can work on C for Change. There are times you have no choice other than to continue in a stressful situation, but you need to change things that are under your control. Change occurs on different levels:

(a) _Attitudes, beliefs and working assumptions._ Maybe you need to change these in order to reduce stress. For example; if you cannot change your toxic work situation, then work on your attitude and appreciate that you are earning a living and receiving a salary every month. You may try and view the angry boss with compassion because he probably has a miserable life, rather than hating him for being angry. This will also help you appreciate your own circumstances – that you can go home to a warm and supportive family or social circle.

(b) *Physical changes.* These can include diet / nutrition, exercise / health care.

(c) *Relaxation.* This might be the biggest gift you give yourself.

Choose the type that is best suited for you, such as deep breathing, yoga or meditation, to name a few. This level of change eats deep into the stress response. It forms an alternative response to habitual stress. It is powerful. It is your friend.

Finally, we end with **E** for Eliminate. This is the most extreme choice, one that is not made often or at the drop of a hat, and it requires much thought and introspection. If you choose to take this step, it is often in your best interest, for your health and for your sanity. Examples are:

1. Moving away from a city

2. Changing jobs

3. Ending a relationship

If a job, a specific relationship or a situation is compromising your health, it is courageous to make the change in the **E** category.

Bottom line.......

➤	*Deal with the issue head-on.*
➤	*Open a file or an app and record the problem and what you feel the possible solutions are.*
➤	*Thereafter, consult with others and then make decisive solutions to try and work yourself out of the seemingly impossible situation you feel trapped in.*

There is another cause for feeling out of control, and that is having too many demands on you at once. There may be too many deadlines and not enough time to attend to them. The cell phone does not stop ringing and people are requesting additional help and tasks to be done.

In this situation, you again must take control.

You must learn to say no, clearly and officially. I always like relating the way my colleagues would say no when I requested them to cover for me when I needed time off work. Initially I was upset, because when they requested the same of me, I would say yes and would make a plan to cover for them. But often I could not manage to do the extra work, and being unclear and indirect made a confusing situation for my colleagues who had relied on me to help out. It is much better to be clear and decline in a nice way if you know that you cannot handle extra work being requested of you.

In addition, you need to make time to wrap up any unfinished tasks. You need to cut out any interference for a certain time period in order to complete the things you need to do.

Examples of taking control:

I have a patient in his 40s who is an estate agent. The housing market is tough, and there are good times and hard times to be had in the market. He was dependent on selling a house from time to time to cover his living expenses. When he ran into a crunch and could not pay the bills, he changed course and took on two jobs. One was in building and the other, that began after four in the afternoon, involved helping to run a catering business. He was earning money but not enough to pay his bills, even though he was working a 12-hour day. He started becoming worn down, and he needed help to get out of a no-win situation where he had lost control. I advised him to meet with a financial advisor to learn how to budget and live within his means, spending only what he had to spend. After a while, we decided he needed one job with a higher salary, which he set out to find at all costs. By spending within his means and finding a job with reasonable hours, he gradually regained control of his finances and could start functioning normally again.

Bottom line.......	
➢	*Learn how to say NO.*
➢	*Work on being decisive in your decisions.*
➢	*Assess whether you can handle a situation or not.*
➢	*Decide if the demand is important and whether you can cope with it.*
➢	*If the answer is NO, then make a firm response that you cannot undertake the task.*

Make sure you have dedicated time to attend to tasks to help you gain control over unfinished business.

Avoid stressful and toxic situations. Do not be pulled into situations where you become more stressed and less in control. Become sensitive and aware of danger signs and avoid getting drawn into conflicts and relationships that are detrimental to you.

Change your attitude in situations that are unalterable and look for the positive in every situation.

If the circumstance is severe and out of control, you may have to make a brave decision in order to get out of the unhealthy situation.

Bottom line.......	
➢	*Simplify the demands.*
➢	*Say no to tasks you cannot undertake.*
➢	*Make time to catch up and complete assignments that you have agreed to do.*

5.2   Completion

A pile of papers in the in-pile on your desk, items on your to-do list, messages in your email and things that are unattended to exacerbate stress. Papers need to be written up and completed, phone calls need to be returned, projects must be finished and there are many other examples of activities that we procrastinate over but need to be tackled. These incomplete tasks are unhealthy and stressful. It is important to set aside uninterrupted time to wrap up unfinished work.

The best approach that I have seen was devised by Dr. Steven Covey in his book *First Things First*. For those readers that recognize not having the ability to complete work as a problem, it is essential to read this book and adopt the principles contained therein.

In essence, you need to set aside blocks of time during the week to complete important work and unfinished tasks. These blocks of time need to be uninterrupted by urgent but less important things. To achieve this, your cell phone should be turned off and you should remain undisturbed for a set amount of time. In this generation where technology has enabled us to be instantly and constantly accessible, whether by cell phone, Whatsapp, Instagram and the like, we are not used to having uninterrupted quiet. However, it is essential to set aside time to be productive and catch up on work that is overdue.

Completing a task is very satisfying. It gives you a sense of accomplishment, aside from freeing you from the pressure of getting the work done. Knowing that there is unfinished work can weigh a person down and result in more time being wasted and further procrastination.

Productivity and reliability can decrease because of the added stress of having to complete certain tasks and not being able to make the time or effort to do so. The subconscious stress of putting things off and knowing that you have to deal with it eventually, although seemingly latent, adds to your stress level and accumulates as time goes by. The greater the vacillation, the more behind you become in your work and the greater the clutter and stress build-up.

Examples of Completing Tasks

I have a patient who is the head of a large educational institution. He is busy with so many tasks and is so overworked and stressed that the direction and the level of the institution is suffering. I advised him to make two sessions in the week of three hours each devoted to completing outstanding issues, uninterrupted. This advice has changed his life.

Another patient of mine who works in a high-tech firm, recently went to meet the CEO of a large organization. Upon entering his office, he was amazed to see that his desk was empty; no papers—not even a telephone—was visible. When he inquired about his clutter-free desk, the CEO responded that his job was to plan and direct his organization, to be organized and efficient. He gives off this impression and has trained his staff accordingly. He seemed quite calm and confident.

Bottom line.......

➤	*Set aside undisturbed time to finish tasks. Make the effort and expend the energy to finish and tie up loose ends — the relief of completion is immeasurable.*
➤	*Make sure you tackle the difficult and unpleasant tasks and don't avoid them. The longer they stay in your in-box, the greater your stress build-up.*
➤	*Get organized.*
➤	*It is helpful to know what needs to be done and to distinguish between urgent tasks and non-urgent ones.*
➤	*Avoid spending unnecessary time on non-critical tasks.*

5.3   Cut Out Toxic Exposure

There are so many influences in life that are not directly connected to an individual and yet become extremely stressful.

This may be in the form of politics, locally or in other countries, the behavior of other people not even remotely connected to you, or news items such as global warming and terrorism. Some of us are addicted to news programs, newspapers and magazines.

37

They are designed for sensational stories and frequently cause stressful reactions in us. Usually you can keep up with essential trends in the world by listening to the news once a week. Most of the time you are hearing or watching the same distressing events brought in more detail and designed to keep our adrenaline pumping.

You need to have a news vacation. Sleeping with your phone under your pillow or near you so that you don't miss out on an important newsflash, should be avoided. It is recommended that not only should you take a day of "disconnect" from your cell phone and computer altogether, but also avoid watching the news for several days in order to take a break from the oppressive news events worldwide.

Another important technique for cutting stress and toxic exposure is by avoiding other extraneous stressors. This may be in the form of a person who is toxic for you or a situation or place that causes you stress. If you can avoid these people or situations, it is important to do so. However, sometimes they cannot be avoided and then having the correct tools and attitude will help you overcome these situations. See the section on attitude.

Bottom line.......

➢	*Limit your time spent with people who cause you unnecessary anxiety. If they are unavoidable, then consider changing your schedule to have less contact with them, or changing your place of contact — for example, your work environment or your neighborhood.*
➢	*If a relationship with someone close to you sours, either try and confront them and change the nature of the relationship or cut your contact with that individual altogether.*
➢	*Avoid things that are not an essential part of your life, but stress you nevertheless, such as the news.*
➢	*Do not become addicted to news sensations or matters that you cannot influence or change. Rather concentrate on things that have a real effect on your life.*

5.4   Concentration

Multitasking may seem like an amazing skill and is often required to help us keep up with the demands placed on us. Some people are more adept at performing multiple tasks at once, but for most of us, it can be quite stressful. The brain must be tuned into a number of tasks at the same time, and one's attention for the single task at hand is reduced.

As a physician, I was always pleased with myself when I could type a report and listen to a patient's complaints whilst at the same time deal with an urgent blood test result. But I have come to realize that the quality of the attention focused on the patient is significantly compromised. This multitasking concept became both stressful and taxing on my brain.

I always admire watching people who are thorough when completing a task and who do it with great attention to detail. They are usually meticulous, productive and do a great job.

It is therefore advisable to concentrate on one thing at a time and let your brain function in a directed and non-stressful way.

A new phenomenon that has developed over the years is wireless communication. We are connected 24/7 — this comes with a price, as we may be missing out on the here and now. Nowadays, it is commonplace to see a couple or friends out to dinner at a restaurant and both parties are so busy texting that they are not even paying any attention to each other. They are engrossed in communicating with others whilst missing out on crucial social interaction around them. It is the same as attending a wedding and being so absorbed in whatsapping photos of the wedding to other people that one misses the wedding itself.

It is paramount to stay focused and become mindful of the situation you are involved in at the present time. Although it requires a lot of work and restraint, it is important to try and limit constant wireless communication, in order to live life to the fullest and stay grounded in the present.

Bottom line.......

➤	*Do what you are good at and do it well!*
➤	*Feel the benefits of focusing on one task at a time and doing it thoroughly.*

5.5 Conflict Avoidance, Conflict Resolution

Who likes to go to bed with unresolved conflicts? When something is bothering you, and in particular when you experience a conflict with another person (whether it is a spouse, neighbor or friend), it is highly likely that you will lie in bed worrying how to avoid the other party, or strategize how to win the battle. A lot of mental energy is wasted contemplating and worrying, resulting in high stress hormone levels.

Wisdom that develops with increasing age teaches us that it is often good to chase a compromise even if we know that we are right. Deciding on a peaceful resolution, even though it may seem that you will come out second best, will actually help you come out ahead, as you gain peace of mind and achieve a relaxed and tranquil composure.

If there is an ongoing conflict that cannot be easily resolved and seems to drain your energy and strength, it is important to take some time to determine a resolution to overcome your stress, anger and frustration. We often tend to avoid dealing with the neighbor who is bothering us or the friend or relation who is being insensitive and hurtful. Addressing these people directly and honestly and dealing with their response until you have resolved the issue will most definitely result in a better feeling on both sides and reduce the tension immediately. I know a woman who never leaves an annoyance or bother unattended to and openly deals with each issue. She heads straight to the person's door to discuss and resolve the issue directly. The truth of the matter is that everyone respects and loves her for this.

Bottom line.......

➢	*Avoid conflict that is not critical to your life.*
➢	*Resolve conflicts quickly before they fester.*
➢	*If a matter is important, deal with the other party in a fair and open way. Always aim for fairness even if you may lose out in the short term. In the long term, you will gain by earning respect and trust, as well as by putting an end to an ongoing conflict.*
➢	*Use compromise as a way to avoid conflict. Aim for a win-win solution where both parties emerge satisfied.*

5.6   Consistency Inside and Consistency Outside

A happy person is someone who is totally consistent with their behavior. They say what it is, and they are what they say.

When a person lives a life of deception and lies, it causes an inconceivable amount of stress. For example, you may want to look more intelligent or younger than you are. It becomes a game of dishonesty and fabrication as you try to conceal the truth, act the part and attempt to project this false image.

In contrast, how different it would be if you would accept who you are and live your life accordingly. Being less wealthy than your neighbor is acceptable, and there is no need to keep up with fancy cars or extravagant clothes. Not having an advanced degree or the best learning skills is acceptable, provided you do the best you can. You need to be satisfied with who you are and not live with hypocrisy and falsehood.

This also extends to speaking authentically. If you talk in circles and fabricate the truth, it increases your stress levels, as no doubt you will need to be on the ball ready to make the next excuse in order to sustain the series of lies and keep the truth from being revealed. At

some point in time it will catch up with you. An example would be if you did something that may upset your spouse and you told a small white lie to cover up the truth. Hiding something that should be shared honestly gnaws at your gut and causes stress overload, especially for fear of the truth being divulged. It is better to consider the consequences of your actions and DON'T DO OR SAY ANYTHING THAT NEEDS YOU TO LIE IN ORDER TO HIDE THE TRUTH.

Someone who is an honest, genuine person, who is straight in their actions, thoughts and words, lives a less complicated and less stressful existence than someone who lives a life of deceit.

Another part of being consistent all around is being reliable. If you give your word, make sure you live up to it. Try your best to always be on time, to pay your debts on time and to arrive at appointments on time. You add unnecessary stress to yourself when you are constantly running late for things and having to play catch-up all day. Being a responsible, reliable person builds self-esteem and makes for easy relationships with people who feel good being around you and are able to rely on you.

Bottom line.......

➢	*Do not do anything that you cannot tell your partner openly and truthfully.*
➢	*Think things through before you act.*
➢	*Do not try and impress others with things that do not belong to you. For example, if you use a clever quote, state who said it.*
➢	*Do not exaggerate — rather say things as they are.*
➢	*Answer questions accurately and honestly. It will make you feel good about yourself and help you speak with confidence. Take the "straight line." Don't do or say anything that you cannot live up to.*

5.7   Creativity and Purpose

Life slips into a different groove if you wake up each morning with a purpose. Starting the day energized and motivated provides a positive energy, and even if you are busy and your day is full, this is a healthy energy and does not cause harmful stress. Knowing that you have some sort of plan for the day brings structure and routine and even reduces stress.

> THE MEANING OF LIFE IS TO FIND YOUR GIFT. THE PURPOSE OF LIFE IS TO GIVE IT AWAY.

Creativity and passion for a project has been found to provide health benefits to the brain and nervous system and, in fact, has been shown to be heart healthy and healthy for the vascular system. The toxic symptoms caused by stress will not be felt with this type of energy.

Making time to spend with family, friends and loved ones helps you develop healthy relationships. Being socially active alleviates stress, especially as the brain releases endorphins when you are happy. This results in a calmer aplomb. Enjoying a relaxing meal or going on an outing with your children — especially in nature — creates positive energy and gives you a good, calm inner feeling.

I addressed the subject of meaning in life in Part II of this book. The essential message is: in order to make our time count and to add lasting value to our lives, **we either have to be building and developing ourselves or contributing to others**. It is very important to select worthwhile activities, set goals and add meaning to our lives, so that we have direction and worthwhile activities to look forward to on an ongoing basis.

Building yourself can include changing career paths or taking courses in areas of interest, self-growth activities or developing new skills.

Developing meaningful relationships by investing time and effort with spouses, children, parents and friends are important ways of giving of yourself to others. Contributing your time and energy to charitable organizations and community services, as well as attempting to improve the life of others by being friendly and helpful, can positively affect everyone around you — as well as yourself.

Bottom line.......

➤	*Never stop looking for meaning in life.*
➤	*Make sure you always have a purpose and worthwhile activities.*
➤	*Work on improving yourself and helping others rather than staying stuck in meaningless, self-centered activities that have no lasting effect.*
➤	*Even when you think you have achieved your life's goals, don't sit back and relax, keep reassessing and repurposing your goals on a daily and long-term basis.*
➤	*Ensure that you wake up in the morning with something worthwhile to achieve.*
➤	*The goals may be small and insignificant, but they are personal and unique tasks, meant only for you.*

CHAPTER 6

More Complicated Matters

We have mentioned how problems need to be resolved and stressors need to be reduced in order to remain in the parasympathetic mode. The above 7C program will not only fundamentally reduce stress, but it will help you see and address various situations in a different light. However, there are times that we must recognize that we cannot overcome certain circumstances on our own, and we must turn to professionals for help.

Seeking Advice

It is important to have a resource of people that you can turn to — to share an issue that seems insurmountable and to obtain good advice. You may turn to a friend who is an experienced businessman for financial advice, or to a religious minister for marriage guidance or parenting advice. Any person who is a good listener and can provide you with sound advice, such as a past college lecturer, a physician or other health practitioner may be helpful. The key is to think things through and have the resourcefulness and often humility to go to someone for help.

Sometimes, it may be necessary to pay for professional help to see a psychologist or financial advisor to get the assistance that you need. It is important to do your research, make the necessary inquiries and find the appropriate person with the right skills and expertise to help you with your problems.

Bottom line.......	
➢	*Have the wisdom and humility to ask for advice and seek help when the solution is not clear to you.*

Attitude

Another essential tool to deal with seemingly overwhelming stressors is having the right attitude.

Attitude is a crucial tool required for taking control of a stressful situation — particularly in areas where you do not have automatic control.

You do have control over how you react in certain circumstances and depending on your attitude, you can allow a bad situation to either affect you negatively or not. You have the ability to choose how you will handle a situation. For example, you have a choice to be bullied and stressed by your boss, or decide that his behavior will not affect you. You can achieve this by doing the best you can in your job, and by being positive and resourceful whilst at the same time ignoring his conduct until you're in a position to change your situation.

You can choose to go to a function that you usually hate attending and decide to make the most of it and ignore the annoying parts.

Any situation that you dislike can either be seen as a punishment or as a challenge to overcome and grow from. It is always in your control to decide what your attitude will be.

Eradicating toxic thought processes that cause anxiety and stress requires work, patience and a change in attitude. Whenever a stressful situation develops, you can either allow your emotions, fears and assumptions to take control, or you can step back and let the rational side of your brain lead the way.

The human brain has the innate ability to "look down" at a situation, almost as if looking at the situation from outside the body — and override the emotional response with a rational response.

We are faced with various challenging situations on a daily basis, and the ability to overcome these challenges successfully depends largely on our attitude.

1. For example, when you go to a party where you know most of the people and you see a couple of unfamiliar faces, it is common practice to judge and get an impression of those individuals — and possibly 'write them off' — before you have even tried to get to know them. Often your prejudice is unjustified and inaccurate.

    Solution: It is best to remain open-minded and adopt a wait-and-see approach. Be open to meeting new people and getting to know them before making a judgment based on superficial feelings.

2. On the flip side of the coin, we have perceptions of ourselves and how people perceive us. We often put up our defense system when amongst other people, so that no one can detect our weaknesses or hurt us. This can prevent us from being warm and friendly, whilst giving the impression of being aloof and defensive.

    Solution: Work on your attitude that you are okay. Accept yourself and recognize that no one is out to get you. You can choose to be warm and open, giving a friendly and welcoming impression. In this way, barriers are eradicated, and new friendships are built.

3. Our disposition is either optimistic or pessimistic. When faced with a challenge, you may rise to the occasion and overcome it or see it as a disaster and lose hope.

In my clinical practice, there are two types of patients. The first type of patient is the one who always has a pessimistic view on things. If a potential problem crops up, such as finding a lump or a mole that has an unusual appearance, they will visualize the worst outcome and become overly stressed, even though the chances of it developing into something serious is slim.

The second type of patient always has a positive attitude and will not become overly concerned about a health issue until it has been proven to be problematic.

The problem with the first type of patient is that their pessimistic outlook initiates a whole set of potential problems and thoughts in the brain. They begin to think of biopsies, tests and surgery that they think will be needed, drawing their minds into a series of stressors that are not even real. The brain launches into survival mode, triggering a cycle of ideas and plans to prevent a serious outcome.

This mindset is totally unnecessary and, more often than not, futile.

Now how can we switch from being a pessimist into an optimist? After all, we cannot lie to our brain. We see some danger in the mole or lump and it could turn out to be serious.

Solution: The first step would be to calm down and make an appointment for a check-up. Don't get caught up in a panic. It is important to stay in a rational mode and understand that there is a much higher chance of a positive outcome than not. Keep your attitude positive and upbeat — it is going to be fine.

4. It is possible to work on and boost your confidence level to help achieve your goals in life and be successful. For example, you may have a general negative feeling about passing an exam or doing well in an interview. This may come from previous failures. If you enable yourself to decide that you are going to succeed, you will tackle your situation with a different attitude. Again, it may be more challenging to deceive your brain if you have failed before, but it is possible to superimpose a positive image over your pessimistic attitude and decide you are going to triumph this time. Be strong! Having a positive attitude will help you achieve great things in life.

Bottom line.......

➤	*In all the above examples, it is possible to rationally influence our attitude.*
➤	*Attitude shifts require a lot of patience and practice.*
➤	*This means that even if you have insecurities and lack confidence, you can influence your behavior by continually shifting your negative attitude to a healthier, optimistic approach.*

A good example of an attitude switch is a doctor who has extreme time restraints not only because he has to see a large number of patients, but he has to be at another clinic by a certain time. He can either watch the clock, hurry through patients and become stressed due to delays incurred by late arrivals and longer appointments. Alternatively, he can decide to spend the necessary time required by each patient, and then deal with running late by either reducing the number of appointments allocated per day, or by just apologizing for his lateness — and continuing to give excellent one-on-one attention to each patient.

Therefore, whenever you feel the pressure of a situation, step back, view the situation with a calm, clear mind and make a rational attitude change.

Another extremely important aspect of feeling more at peace and relaxed is to seek spiritual guidance. Those of you who recognize that life is not in the hands of man and who turn to a higher power — submitting yourself and asking for help — will enjoy immense relief and a sense of comfort. This enables you to do your best in any given situation, as you recognize that your job is to do the correct thing and expend the required effort — and the rest is not up to you. You can rely on your Maker for help, and you can stop pushing and accept the outcome.

An example is a person's income. You may think that there is no limit to how long and how hard you can work to earn more money. Alternatively, you can accept that there is a limit to how much you can earn no matter how many hours you put in. You may earn more and lose the extra earnings by paying taxes or an unexpected bill.

Your attitude is all about seeing the cup half full as opposed to half empty. In other words, you can see the same situation with two different lenses. Even if things are not going very well, they could be worse. You should try and maintain a positive attitude in all situations.

A typical example is a patient of mine who is in his late 60s. He relied on his job for his monthly income and was hoping to get a promotion that was being offered in his company. When he didn't get it, he started seeing things in a negative light, and soon thereafter, he resigned. He started another job that turned out to be far worse, and he was eventually fired. Fortunately, he was rehired at his former company, and with a change in his attitude, he was able to see things through a more positive lens.

Appreciation is central to living a calmer life. If you feel like everything is owed to you as opposed to being a giver, then you will never be satisfied. You will always have high expectations and believe that you deserve everything, whether from the government, school or any other institution, or from your spouse or a friend. However, if you start appreciating what you have, even the small things, then you put an end to your feelings of anger, resentment and disappointment.

You should start by trying to give and contribute to others. This may sound strange, but by changing your disposition to be a giver and not always expecting and taking from others, you will alter your demeanor and be much more satisfied and relaxed. It is worth a try.

The truth is there really is a lot to be grateful for, even for those of you who are going through a rough time. You can miss out on appreciating the small things even when there are big things weighing down on you. Look around. Open yourself up to appreciating what you have been given, and not only in material terms. You are surrounded by the beauty of nature. Enjoy it. Savor the tastes of your food. Acknowledge people who help you. These are all things to notice and not take for granted, lest you remain stuck in your own self-centered world, which can be depressing and make things worse for you.

Attitude is a vital part of building ourselves. It is something that we have control over. Working on developing a healthy attitude plays a huge role in our lives not only in how we conduct ourselves in various situations, but also on our overall health.

Bottom line.......

➢	*Choose the correct attitude to handle a stressor. Make a potentially unpleasant situation into a challenge and an area of personal growth — and not something that pulls you down and possibly destroys you.*

I would now like to present an approach to managing anxiety, as this ignites stress hormones and is a major cause of stress.

Essentially anxiety and phobias are caused by the brain perceiving a real threat to a person. A classic example would be a soldier on patrol in a hostile village in Afghanistan. The enemy could be hiding in any house overlooking the alley that he is patrolling. Any false move could trigger a volley of enemy fire and possibly mean the end of his life. The fear experienced by this soldier is a REAL fear.

Now let us take a person who has a fear of flying. He imagines the potential of something going wrong and envisions the plane plummeting to the earth. This is such a vivid reality to him that he feels the fear in the same way that soldier fears for his life, as described above. The only difference is that the soldier's angst has a higher probability of occurring, whereas the chances of the plane crashing is extremely unlikely.

The anxious person visualizes the worst-case scenario even though there is no need to entertain these thoughts in the first place. When you start perceiving unlikely possibilities as being real, we have the same fear of disaster as the real thing and the brain's perception of this fear and the subsequent stress response will be identical. The brain will not distinguish if the fear is real or not. Our reaction is largely dependent on how we view and control this fear.

Often when it comes to medical issues, many patients immediately fear the worst outcome. Finding a swollen lymph node automatically means cancer to some, whilst others will regard the same lymph node as not being very significant and unlikely to lead to anything.

Therefore, the difference in how anxious you may become is not dependent on if you are a hero or not, but rather on how REAL you perceive the "danger" to be in a particular situation. The oversensitive, negative person is going to sense disaster even when it is not there, as opposed to another person who will look at the positive side and feel that there is no real danger.

It is obvious that if we can train ourselves not to feel all the possible dangers and consequences of a situation and instead be POSITIVE, we would save ourselves from a lot of anxiety and anguish. This process requires work. You need to visualize that the plane trip will be safe and do not allow any thoughts of disaster to enter your mind. You have to work on being positive. Whatever the medical diagnosis is, you are going to be okay.

Stop looking up all the disastrous possibilities on the internet. In my experience, the "Googlers" are almost never right and they experience extreme anxiety with what they have discovered as their "diagnosis." A lot of the time, their information is imprecise, and their diagnosis is incorrect.

Keep pushing your brain to see the positive outcome, and don't look for potential disasters. If there is a REAL risk, like crossing a wobbly bridge over a deep ravine, just don't cross it.

A crucial aspect of anxiety is the fear of the anxiety attack itself. Anyone who has experienced an anxiety attack knows how frightening it is. It is so unpleasant, that even if you do not think of the possible risks of doing something, you become anxious from the possibility of getting anxious or panicky and experiencing an anxiety attack. In other words, the fear of the feeling of anxiety that will occur becomes the main problem, even if you are not so fearful of doing the actual activity.

It is crucial to understand that as unpleasant as it is to experience the anxiety attack, it is not dangerous and it will pass with time. The big block against doing something or going somewhere is the actual fear of having an attack. Instead of trying to stop it from happening, you need to learn how to accept the discomfort and go with it. It will not affect your health, and the more you can embrace this fact, the less it will bother you; eventually, it may disappear altogether.

I have seen that reassuring a person that there are no health risks involved usually helps lessen the actual fear of the attack. You have to go with the anxiety and not fight it. If it begins, it is okay. You need to just breathe deeply, go with the flow and let it run its course. With time, you will calm down and it will disappear. Even though feeling apprehensive is unpleasant, if you can accept it and not fear it, especially as it is harmless, you will lessen your fear and anxiety.

There are situations where the anxiety reaction becomes somewhat embarrassing and will become obvious to others. An example is someone who stutters, and anxiety may make the stutter more pronounced. Or someone who has a fear of giving a presentation, and he may lose his breath and breathe unevenly. The anxiety then becomes his fear of revealing this so-called weakness that is often beyond his control.

I have heard from people in this situation that it is best to come to terms with this so-called weakness and feel comfortable and confident in front of others. Imagine you are about to deliver a talk to a large audience and you suddenly think back to your previous attempt where you struggled to breathe, your heart was pounding in your throat and it was obvious that everyone noticed how anxious you were.

This fear of the audience noticing your vulnerability can arouse the same uneasiness and cause you to panic again. It is a physiological reaction beyond your control. There are two ways to resolve your fear: one is to try and talk yourself into calming down, and the other is to share your feelings with the audience if it occurs and admit that you get quite anxious with public speaking. Take a drink of water or tell a joke to try and break the ice a little, and then continue your presentation hopefully with a little more confidence. By taking control of your feelings, it will allow you to eventually overcome your anxiety.

Conversely, if you do not make peace with your weakness by accepting and embracing it, you will continue to feel anxious and embarrassed.

Anxiety can be debilitating for some people and can affect many areas of your life, such as not wanting to travel to other places for fear of flying. If you find that trying to calm yourself down on your own is impossible, then seek professional help to give you the tools you need to strengthen and help you overcome your fears.

Self-Esteem

We all have basic physiological and psychological needs. In fact, Abraham Maslow first introduced this concept of a hierarchy of needs in his 1943 paper, "A Theory of Human

Motivation." This hierarchy suggests that people require certain fundamental needs to be met before moving onto more advanced needs. By fulfilling an individual's basic requirements, it encourages them to move on to the next level in the pyramid.

People have an inborn desire to be self-actualized — that is, to be the best that they can be. However, in order to achieve this, a few basic needs must first be met, such as the need for food and love. This is followed by a need for safety, then a need for belonging and finally, self-esteem and self-actualization.

Self-esteem can be described as your overall sense of self-worth or self-respect, and it plays a large role in your ability to succeed in life. Too little self-esteem can leave you feeling defeated or depressed and can result in bad life choices, such as becoming involved in destructive relationships. It can also hold you back from becoming successful at work or in school because you don't have the confidence to move forward and be an achiever; rather, you feel worthless and inadequate. This lack of self-esteem can prevent you from reaching your full potential.

Too much self-esteem, such as can be seen in people suffering from narcissistic personality disorder, can be destructive to personal relationships and can be quite off-putting to others. Some of the behavior characterized by an overly self-centered individual includes:

- A constant need for attention, praise and affirmation

- A belief that they are "special" and can only associate with people of the same status
- An exaggerated sense of their own achievements and abilities
- Exploiting other people for personal gain
- A preoccupation with power and success
- Feeling that other people are envious of them, or they are envious of others
- A lack of empathy for others

A person with low self-esteem usually depicts himself in a negative light, and usually feels somewhat inferior to others. Signs of a low self-esteem include:

- A negative general outlook
- A lack of confidence
- An inability to express their needs
- Feelings of shame, anxiety or depression
- Belief that others are better than them
- Focus on their weaknesses and what they are lacking
- Resistance to accepting positive feedback
- Fear of failure

High and low ends of the scale can be harmful, so it is best to strike a balance somewhere in the middle. A realistic yet positive view of yourself is generally considered the ideal. Signs of a healthy self-esteem are as follows:

- Confidence
- A positive outlook on life
- The ability to say no

- The ability to see your overall strengths and weaknesses and to accept them
- The ability to express your needs
- Empathy for others
- Negative experiences do not impact your overall perspective

There are many factors that affect your self-esteem. Genetic factors play a role in shaping your overall personality, however, life experiences often form the basis for self-esteem. A person who constantly receives negative criticism or negative judgments from peers, family members or friends, will most likely suffer from low self-esteem. Hearing negative comments on an ongoing basis will mold how you see yourself and how you perceive what others think of you.

Other factors that can also have an impact on you include your maturity, disabilities, physical limitations and your vocation.

People are usually aware of what they are capable of. If you write a test in mathematics and you get a low score, whereas everyone else gets a high score, you will no doubt feel a lack of intelligence. A parent cannot convince a child that he is bright when in fact he is battling with his tests and receiving low grades.

In this regard, it would be more productive to shift the child's focus away from his negative abilities and focus on his strengths and areas where he can achieve. A feeling of strength and triumph as a result of his success will enhance his self-esteem. Adding small challenges in weaker areas will help strengthen him through hard work, patience and subsequent success. The combination of realizing his talents and succeeding slowly in challenging areas will build self-esteem.

People with poor self-esteem will always feel bad and overly stressed in any challenging situation. They are never satisfied with their accomplishments and often bring other people down, due to frustration.

It is important to build up low self-esteem. Seek professional help if need be, as this psychological need is crucial to a person's success in life, how they view themselves and the world around them.

Personality Type

Stress is a major cause of coronary heart disease. Extensive research has been done to determine how your personality type affects the way you handle stress. Doctors Meyer Friedman and Ray Rosenman, both cardiologists, discovered the Type A personality by studying their patients' behavioral patterns in their waiting room. It seemed that the upholstery on their waiting room chairs oddly needed to be reupholstered on the arms of the chairs, as opposed to the usual seat part.

This led to further personality studies and the division into contrasting personality types; namely type A and B personalities.

Type A individuals are outgoing, ambitious, highly status-conscious, proactive and concerned with time management. They tend to be rigidly organized, very competitive and self-critical and strive towards goals without feeling a sense of joy in their efforts or accomplishments. Akin to this is the presence of a life imbalance characterized by high work involvement, more job-related stress and less job satisfaction. Type A personalities push themselves with deadlines, disliking both delays and uncertainty. These individuals tend to overreact and are easily aroused to anger or hostility, displaying envy and sometimes a lack of compassion. Additional character traits include impulsiveness, hastiness, impatience and anger.

Doctor Friedman observed three different areas that expressed the type A personality, including (1) free floating hostility that could be triggered by minor incidents; (2) time urgency and impatience, that causes irritation and exasperation; and (3) a competitive drive that causes stress and an achievement-driven mentality. These individuals are also more likely to experience higher levels of stress and high blood pressure.

Type B individuals on the other hand, are a direct contrast to type A. They work steadily, and although they are content when they achieve something, it is not their end-goal. Type B personalities disregard physical and mental stress and take their time mulling over situations. When faced with competition, they focus less on winning or losing and more on the enjoyment of the game. Type B personalities are more drawn to creative careers that explore ideas and concepts such as writers, counselors, therapists or actors/actresses.

Individuals with a type B personality are more easy-going. They are not affected when they do not meet their goals and are not afraid to fail. In the work environment they are less competitive, preferring a comfortable work experience over success, and are more balanced with regard to their work and family life. Generally, type B personalities are innovative and love to explore concepts and ideas.

Individuals who experience higher stress levels have a greater tendency to develop various illnesses. A person with a type A personality can help minimize their chances of developing illnesses by doing the following:

1. Try to relax and slow down once in a while. Try to avoid extreme competitiveness that inevitably leads to stress.

2. Relaxation is very important, that no one gets from working consistently. Be mindful of a healthy balance between work and your private life.

3. Make sure to accommodate your need for immediate recognition to achieve.

4. Make sure when starting a project that you have enough time to finish it, so that even if you are under pressure to finish it, you will not get frustrated and angry whilst trying to complete the task timeously.

5. Delegate tasks when necessary — don't try and do everything yourself.

6. Make time for your family — take a vacation once in a while!

7. Talk about your feelings and goals with people who are close to you. This helps reduce stress and anxiety.

8. Make sure that you set realistic goals for yourself and revisit them regularly. This will help you to continually reach your goals and won't overburden you with unrealistic ambitions. The frustration of pushing yourself and achieving what you set out to do is the dangerous aspect of a type A personality.

That being said, individuals do not necessarily fit into any one particular "box," and having a specific personality may not mean you will definitely develop heart disease or any other illness. More up-to-date research shows that a type A personality type alone does not necessarily lead to an increased risk of heart disease. These individuals can be quite healthy, can be achievers and can feel fulfilled. However, character traits that display greater anger levels, hostility and the inability to cope with stress, are higher risk factors for developing illnesses. The combination of Type A personality, frustration, anger and stress makes a toxic mix that can become quite dangerous.

More on Adrenal Fatigue

Adrenal fatigue was first discovered by Dr. James L. Wilson, who recognized that there was a syndrome of low adrenal gland function, other than Addison's disease.

Conventional medicine recognizes two conditions associated with the adrenal gland and cortisol production. As I mentioned before, the adrenal gland produces a few hormones, but the main hormone involved in the chronic stress response is cortisol. When very low cortisol levels are produced, it is called Addison's disease and is as a result of damage to the adrenal gland. If too much cortisol is produced, this is called Cushing's disease.

However, what if high or low cortisol occurs but not at the levels of Addison's or Cushing's disease? Conventional medicine would not consider these levels to be abnormal and would therefore not administer any treatment.

Dr. Wilson demonstrates how adrenal fatigue evolves. Initially, elevated stress levels cause high cortisol levels. If this continues, then cortisol begins to drop. This leads to fatigue and the inability to handle even the smallest stressors in life.

Cortisol levels fluctuate throughout the day. Usually the highest amounts are found at 8 a.m. when you have recovered after a good night's rest, and slowly reduces during the course of the day until it reaches the lowest level at around 11 p.m. at night.

Saliva tests are an accurate way of testing cortisol levels. Saliva is collected in little ampules four times in a day — at 8 a.m., 11 a.m., 4 p.m. and 11 p.m. and are sent to the laboratory where they plot the levels on a curve. Initially, with high stress, cortisol will be high, which makes you feel wired, edgy and unable to sleep. The cortisol levels will be above the normal curve. Treatment will require stress management and supplements that lower cortisol levels, such as Relora and phosphatidyl serine.

In the next phase, cortisol levels will decrease, which causes you to become weak and exhausted and unable to deal with life. It becomes difficult to get started in the morning and by the afternoon, you are ready to collapse.

These patterns are recognized by the salivary test results that show low cortisol levels, yet conventional physicians do not test for this or even recognize the problem. These patterns on the graph correlate well with people's symptoms and are clear proof of the existence of the syndrome called adrenal fatigue. The treatment for suppressed cortisol levels is different from high levels. Rest and recovery are a must and I recommend supplements that contain ashwagandha, licorice and rhodiola.

Adrenal fatigue is not only a fascinating syndrome, but it is very common. We need to recognize it and treat it because it can have a ripple effect on other symptoms that you experience and may cause complications in other areas of your health.

The Frazzle Factor

The brain has a certain capacity to weather attrition. It is almost like building blocks, with each new stressor adding an additional block onto the pile. If not strengthened, at a certain point the foundation will eventually become unstable and start cracking, and finally crumble.

An example is a businessman who is trying to hold his shaky business together. In addition to this problem, he has an ill parent who needs to get to the hospital daily, and an adolescent son experiencing teenage issues. All these attritions add up to a constant battering of the brain. Without reducing some of his stressors, there is no hope to help him overcome his anxiety and ongoing stress.

Therefore, the first step it to try and cut down on the amount of frazzle that is occurring. By this, I mean decreasing the stress onslaught from different areas. Hand over some of the overwhelming responsibilities to another capable person. In the above example, asking his wife or friend to help out with rides to the hospital and getting help for is teenage son would take an enormous weight off his shoulders.

If your input is putting more pressure on a situation, it is better to withdraw and work on keeping a calm demeanor. Pulling out of multiple stressors can give you space to recover a bit, assess the circumstances and make rational decisions. Just because you take a step back does not mean you need to exclude yourself altogether. Giving yourself the necessary time and space to recoup your equanimity, is sometimes required to help you get through a difficult patch in your life.

Bottom line.......

➤	*The brain can only take so much onslaught until it passes the frazzle limit and stops functioning rationally.*
➤	*Decrease the stressors and take some time to recover before tackling your problems one step at a time.*

CHAPTER 7

Stress Management Techniques

I began this book by emphasizing that it is essential to handle stress from the root causes by determining the issues at hand and then working to eradicate them. This enables you to switch on the parasympathetic nervous system and increase vagal tone. However, there is value in adopting stress reduction techniques that work as an interim strategy and can be used to immediately alleviate symptoms while you are working on the bigger picture.

No one is created equal, and each stress relief technique works differently for every person. When choosing the right method for you, take into consideration your lifestyle, fitness level, how you react to stress and what approach would best help you interrupt your stressful thoughts and bring about calm and serenity to your overall being. Sitting in front of a TV screen might take your mind away from the stressors of the day but will do little to reduce the harmful effects of continuous stress and bring about the body's natural relaxation response.

Your relaxation choice will largely depend on the way you react in a stressful situation.

- **The "fight" response.** If you are more likely to be bothered, upset, edgy or uptight, the best stress relief techniques for you would be to calm your body down through meditation, deep breathing, progressive muscle relaxation or guided imagery.
- **The "flight" response.** If you are more likely to become depressed, discouraged, withdrawn, or spacey, the best stress relief techniques for you would be activities that are stimulating and invigorate your nervous system, such as rhythmic exercise, massage, mindfulness or yoga.
- **The immobilization response.** If you have experienced a traumatic ordeal in the past and your reaction in a stressful situation is to freeze up, your first step in relaxing would be to stimulate your nervous system into a fight-or-flight response so that your body will calm down. To do this, choose a physical activity that uses both your arms and legs, such as running, dancing, yoga or tai chi and concentrate carefully on the sensations in your limbs as you move.

Below are some recommended techniques that should be adopted according to your body's stress response. The first five techniques will assist with reigniting the vagus nerve. You want your vagus nerve to be activated in order to positively influence the many systems of the body. Even if you work on reducing the core causes of stress by going through the 7C program, it is still beneficial to practice techniques that will increase vagal tone.

a) Deep breathing techniques

Deep breathing techniques help reduce stress, relaxing you and even exchanging feelings of fear and anger for calm and confidence. It has several additional health benefits, including treatment for sleep problems, anxiety disorders and general aches and pains.

These exercises are perfected with practice and can be performed at home, whilst on the train to work or even at your office desk. They don't take long to do but can have an incredibly calming effect to help you get through your day. Deep breathing can also be combined with meditation and guided imagery, as well as aromatherapy and meditative music.

It is a fact that when one breathes in, there is increased sympathetic tone in order to speed up the pulse and push more blood to the lungs to receive oxygen. When exhaling, the vagus tone increases in order to slow the heart and make it more efficient. This variability in pulse is called Heart Rate Variability (HRV). If the vagus tone is weak and there is no slowing of the heart rate, then the sympathetic nerve remains dominant, which is not healthy and may even be dangerous. Conscious breathing helps to stimulate vagal tone.

When doing the exercise below, you should be cognizant of your breathing, with each breath being slow and calculated.

- Sit up straight with your feet together or lie flat on the floor with your legs slightly raised. You can keep your eyes open or closed during this exercise.
- Place one hand on your chest and the other on your stomach.
- Breathe in through your nose — your hand on your stomach should rise whilst the hand on your chest should not.
- Breathe out slowly through your mouth — again the hand on your stomach should fall whilst the hand on your chest should barely move.
- Repeat whilst slowing allowing your whole body to relax. If you find it difficult to breathe from your

abdomen in this position, try lying on your back and placing a book on your stomach instead.

b) *Rhythmic exercise*

Rhythmic exercise is exercise that uses both your arms and legs, such as walking, running, swimming, cycling, dancing etc. The best way to maximize the effects of this technique is to be mindful whilst doing them. In other words, concentrate intensely on the how your body feels, your actions and sensations — how it feels when your foot touches the ground or your knees bend whilst running. Try not to let your mind wander onto other thoughts, but to stay focused purely on the actions and feelings of your body.

c) Cold showers or cold water on the face

Any acute cold exposure will increase vagal tone, such as taking a cold shower or dipping your face in cold water.

d) Singing or chanting

Singing, humming and mantra chanting all increase heart rate variability (HRV). They work the muscles at the back of your throat that helps activate the vagus nerve.

e) Gargling

Gargling with a glass of water or salt water each morning will help contract the muscles at the back of the throat. This in turn helps to activate the vagus nerve.

f) Tongue depressor

Tongue depressors stimulate the gag reflex. This is similar to gargling or humming as they stimulate reflexes mediated by the vagus nerve.

g) Progressive relaxation technique

This technique involves tensing and then relaxing different muscles in the body in an orderly fashion, starting from your toes and working your way up to your head. It entails tensing a group of muscles and holding it for the count of 5 and then relaxing to the count of ten.

Begin by tensing your toes on your right foot and putting all your attention and concentration into this action. Then move up to your right calf. After tensing and relaxing it, continue onto your thigh before repeating the exercises with your left leg. Follow on to your abdominal muscles, the buttocks, gluteal muscles and your arms before finishing off with your mouth and forehead.

Whilst performing these exercises, make sure you concentrate only on the area of your body that you are tensing. This ensures that random brain waves are reduced and a more rhythmic firing of the brain neurons occurs, which helps relax the mind and body. This relaxation method also puts you in touch with how your body feels when it is stressed and tense and makes you aware of how it feels to relieve the tension. As your body relaxes, so does your mind.

h) Visualization meditation (guided imagery)

Visualization meditation is very relaxing and can even put you to sleep. It not only requires you to picture yourself in a different setting, but it incorporates the use of all five senses whilst allowing a calmness to wash over your body. When using guided imagery, make sure you choose a location that is appealing and relaxing to you and not what is accepted as the norm, such as the beach.

- Find a cool, quiet place where you can sit and close your eyes.
- Picture a setting that is pleasant and restful to you.
- Make use of all five senses whilst exploring your surroundings. For example:

- Walk through a magnificent forest with a stream
- Listen to the birds chirping and the water rippling down the stream

- Smell fresh moss growing on the ground and the clean, crisp air
- Feel the soft moss under your feet and the cool water flowing through your hands
- Watch the sun sparkling through the trees and lighting up all the different plants and flowers
- Taste the sweet, clear, cold water in the stream
- Let your imagination flow and when you feel rested and calm, slowly open your eyes and stretch.
- You can listen to music at the same time to help you unwind further.

i) Yoga and Tai Chi

Although different in their techniques, yoga, tai chi and

qigong comprise a series of different movements and body positions — all focusing on building strength, balance, stamina and causing energy to flow through your body, whilst at the same time promoting relaxation, the release of stress and anxiety and bringing about calm to your overall being.

These exercises should be performed with a trained professional in order to avoid any injuries and to ensure the maximum benefit.

j) Healthy sleep

Poor sleep patterns could mean waking up several times during the night or sleeping for a few hours and then lying awake watching the time tick by. Lack of sleep not only depletes your energy levels, but also affects your ability to function during the day, your mood and your working ability. Most experts agree that between 7 to 9 hours is the ideal amount of sleep time required per night, but a person's age, health, lifestyle and physical activeness impacts the amount of sleep that is required by an individual.

Most people experience insomnia sometime during their lifetime, which can be categorized into primary or secondary, acute or chronic. Primary insomnia is defined as sleep issues unrelated to any health conditions, whereas secondary insomnia is usually as a result of a medical problem, for example; asthma, heartburn, arthritis, pain or side effects from medication.

Insomnia is classified as either acute (short-term) or chronic (long-term), depending on how long it lasts. Stress and anxiety play a key role in causing both acute and chronic insomnia, which could be the result of a highly stressful occurrence, such as the loss of a job, divorce or death of a loved one.

The body requires uninterrupted, quality sleep to repair itself. Research has indicated that an ongoing lack of sleep can cause increased levels of cortisol production. Ongoing elevated levels results in inflammation and can lead to more serious illnesses.

Below are a few pointers to enable you to realize a good night's sleep:

- Ensure that the room is cool, quiet and dark. An important sleep-regulating hormone called melatonin is produced by the brain but is affected by even a small amount of light.
- Enforce a regular sleep routine by going to sleep and waking up at more or less the same time each day. Wind down at bedtime by reading, listening to music or taking a warm bath.
- It is preferable to avoid an adrenaline rush first thing in the morning. Therefore, turn off computers, smartphones and other devices that might trigger a shock to your system and place them at least 10 feet away from the bed.
- Avoid adrenal stimulants that impose excessive stress on the adrenal glands, such as sugary foods and caffeine — especially at night-time — and can interfere with sleep patterns. Nicotine and alcohol also have an adverse effect on sleep.
- Our cortisol levels are lowest at night and it is therefore best to go to sleep before 10p.m. so as not to push our body beyond its natural limits.

- A light protein snack before bedtime can help promote sleep — for example, a handful of nuts or cottage cheese.
- If you have trouble falling asleep, try and do some breathing exercises or relaxation techniques and go back to bed when you are tired. Don't agonize over falling asleep, it creates added stress.

k) Healthy nutrition

The type of food you eat definitely impacts how you feel.

 When we are stressed, we tend to miss meals or reach for an unhealthy snack such as chocolate, macaroni and cheese, crackers or even fast food, that fills us up with carbohydrates and sugars. This may give us a temporary lift, and even a slight sugar high, but does little for our body weight. Sugar levels soon drop, leaving us feeling lethargic and less able to deal with stress.

It is extremely important to be vigilant when it comes to eating healthily, especially when you are feeling stressed and anxious. Stress causes cortisol levels to rise, which in turn causes food cravings — especially in women. Therefore, the best choices are foods and snacks that are rich in nutrients and at the same time have a calming effect on your system, such as berries, grass fed beef, nuts and oranges, to name a few. They do not add extra calories but rather give you the energy you need to get through the day, and at the same time, they calm you down. Below are some other ways to improve your nutrition and help reduce your stress levels:

- Make sure you sit down when eating a meal and do not "eat on the run." Eating in a calm setting helps aid digestion and decreases stress-induced symptoms, such as abdominal pain and headaches.
- Reduce your high glycemic index carbohydrate intake by substituting white flour, pastas, rice and potatoes for whole grain flour, whole grain pastas and sweet potatoes.
- Reduce your sugars, fizzy drinks and alcohol by substituting herbal and green teas instead. Drink plenty of water, and add a piece of lemon for a refreshing flavor.
- Substitute processed foods for chicken, meat, fish and legumes. Make sure you eat enough protein daily.
- Eat plenty of fresh fruits and vegetables.

l) Exercise

Often when you are stressed and overwhelmed, exercise is the farthest thing from your mind and something that you make little time for. However, incorporating exercise into your daily routine can go a long way to helping you overcome anxiety and improve your stress management. When you exercise, the brain releases feel-good neurotransmitters, called endorphins, that give you an overall sense of well-being.

Doing physical exercise, such as walking, swimming, playing tennis or aerobics, helps you focus on the activity at hand and moves your concentration away from the stressors affecting you. Exercise also has the added benefit of improving your sleep, your mood, mild depression and anxiety. It is recommended that you do around 150 minutes of mild to vigorous exercise per week, which will not only help reduce your stress level, but keep your body in shape and enhance your self -image.

A word of caution, however: exercising without adequate breaks can increase the stress placed on your system and will deplete your stress hormones even further, which could lead to adrenal fatigue. You should alternate between high intensity exercise and sessions of lower intensity or different types of exercises. A good program may be aerobic interval training 3–4 times a week and two sessions of strength training in between.

m) Heart rate variability (HRV)

This concept is central to understanding the stress effects on your body and will also provide a very useful mechanism to reduce stress in the long term. For this reason, it is worth taking some time to understand the concept.

The heartbeat is controlled by an electrical impulse that is initiated in a little node in the heart muscle called the sinoatrial node. This node fires an electrical impulse that spreads through the heart muscle and causes the heart to contract. This electrical impulse would normally be very regular, meaning that the time between each beat is exactly the same.

However, the two nervous systems that we are familiar with by now (parasympathetic and sympathetic) are connected to this node and influence its beat. If sympathetic influence is dominant, then the beat will become very regular and the time between each heartbeat is identical. If parasympathetic influence becomes dominant, then there will be a slight variability in the heartbeat and the time between each pulse is not exactly the same, which is preferred.

I described earlier how inhalation is affected by the sympathetic nerve and exhalation by the vagus nerve, and that if the vagal tone is prevalent when we breathe out, the heart rate slows down. A stressed individual will not have the vagal tone to slow down the heart and will only have a sympathetic influence. This results in the heart rate being very regular with not much heart rate variability.

The variation in heartbeat is evident in fetuses in utero who are under distress. Their heartbeat becomes very regular, whereas when they were thriving and doing well the heartbeat is less regular.

Therefore, stress makes the heart beat evenly with minimal heart rate variability, whereas a relaxed mode will result in a slightly uneven heartbeat, as can be seen in infants, children and young adults who for the most part have a slightly uneven beat. Poor heart rate variability is associated with a number of health risks, including the elevated risk of a heart attack, sudden death after a heart attack, diabetes, and the overall risk for earlier death and decreased longevity.

The HRV can be measured using various devices. The score that is obtained can indicate if you are in a relaxed mode — which will give a good heart rate variability — or in a stressed mode — which would result in a low heart rate variability.

As we mentioned, people don't always recognize the physiological signs of stress, but increased awareness can cultivate a more mindful attitude, enabling you to become aware of what may cause stress. This awareness will empower you to avoid certain situations and change your habits. You can also apply one of the stress reduction techniques to reduce stress and increase the HRV.

The following lifestyle choices are known to increase HRV, including:

- Yoga
- Techniques to increase vagal tone
- Meditation
- Acupuncture
- Nutrition — eating whole foods and eliminating foods that can cause an allergic reaction
- Natural products that help to relieve stress

Medical drugs used for treating stress and anxiety all come with side effects and should only be used under a physician's guidance when decidedly indicated.

There are many natural products on the market with claims that they help relieve stress and anxiety. Not all of them are effective. Below is a list of natural products that have proven to be effective and are recommended for their efficacy and safety.

These products are suitable for adrenal fatigue to help the adrenal glands recover. They are helpful in situations where a person suffers from adrenal fatigue or burnout due to prolonged stress, being overworked and the inability to cope with everyday life.

Adrenal Fatigue Supplements

Adaptogens are a group of herbal ingredients that have the unique ability to "adapt" their function according to the body's needs. In particular, they are used to improve your adrenal health, which is the system that manages your hormonal response to stress, enabling you to fight fatigue and cope with anxiety and stress. Although the effects of these herbs are subtle at first, over time, they make a real difference to your body and overall well-being.

Rhodiola Root Extract — This is an adaptogenic herb that has been shown to combat fatigue and restore energy to the body. It is ideal for building physical and mental resistance to stress. It is  useful in blocking the depletion of noradrenaline and dopamine that typically occurs in stressful situations. Rhodiola's working mechanism also assists neurotransmitter transport in the brain and the blunting of catecholamine release.

 **Siberian Ginseng** — Not to be confused with other varieties of ginseng, this herb is also an adaptogen, used to support and rejuvenate adrenal function. It enhances immunity, sustains endurance, and improves social functioning and energy levels. Studies by the University of Maryland Medical Center have shown that Siberian Ginseng strengthens the body's ability to cope with stress and reduces stress-related medical conditions such as heartburn, tension headaches and abdominal pain.

Ashwagandha — Another adaptogenic herb, ashwagandha has powerful rejuvenating abilities and has helped patients resist stress and reduce anxiety, almost in the same way as alcohol. This herb is noted for its ability to balance out thyroid and adrenal problems and has been used to help hypofunction in both of these energy-producing glands. Ashwagandha has been shown to relieve insomnia and stress-induced depression, as well as reduce cortisol  concentrations and the immunosuppressive effects of stress.

Licorice Deglycerized — Licorice is a well-known herb for supporting adrenal function. It helps decrease the breakdown or metabolism of hydrocortisone by the liver. This in turn increases cortisol in circulation and reduces the strain on the adrenal glands to produce it. It is also known to increase energy, endurance and vitality, as well as stimulate the adrenal hormones for anti-inflammatory action. Licorice is suitable  for those individuals who have reached the exhaustion stage and are experiencing fatigue due to chronic stress and low cortisol levels.

Vitamin B6 and B12 — B complex vitamins are important vitamins that act as coenzymes in various biochemical 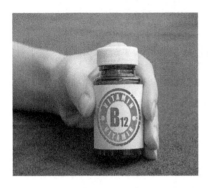 reactions in cells and regulate many processes in the body, such as cell metabolism. They assist in the production of various hormones in the adrenal gland including cortisol, adrenaline, aldosterone, estrogen and testosterone, which help the body cope with stress. A deficiency in B vitamins leads to low energy levels and increased fatigue.

The following natural products help relieve anxiety:

Lemon balm — Lemon balm is a member of the mint family and is considered a calming herb. It has been used for hundreds of years to reduce stress and anxiety, promote sleep, improve appetite, and ease pain and  discomfort from indigestion, such as gas, bloating and colic. In years gone by, it was steeped in wine to heal wounds and treat venomous bites and stings. Today, lemon balm is often combined with other calming, soothing herbs, such as valerian, chamomile and hops to promote relaxation.

L-Theanine — L-Theanine is an amino acid that has a calming effect without sedating. It is found in green tea and is

harmonious with caffeine in that it has the ability to "take the edge off." L-Theanine helps reduce the perception of stress and, with its relaxation capabilities, it can assist a person with sleep issues.

Holy Basil Leaf — It has been demonstrated that Holy Basil Leaf can reduce anxiety and depression, as well as physical and emotional stress. The herb helps reduces the amount of cortisol released during a stressful period and acts as an adaptogen, managing acute and chronic stress and fatigue.

Passionflower — Passionflower is sometimes used in conjunction with lemon balm as a treatment for anxiety and insomnia. Researchers discovered that passionflower

increases the levels of the chemical called gamma aminobutyric acid (GABA) in the brain, which is responsible for lowering activity in certain brain cells, creating a calm, relaxed feeling.

DOWNTIME

It is very important to incorporate some relaxation time in your busy schedule in order to refresh your brain and your emotions. You need to get off the roller coaster of life and take time off to do some things that you enjoy doing. Venturing into nature is often a great relaxer. Going on a hike in the nearest nature park or driving through the mountains has an automatic calming effect. Listening to the sounds in nature and observing the colors and wonders of the natural environment will immediately bring about a calm feeling and put you in a relaxed mood.

If you cannot go on a long vacation, aim for shorter ones to break up your long work schedule. Taking short vacations can revive your soul. It can be as little as three days, but just changing your surroundings can make a difference to how you feel.

I worked with a very busy pediatrician who was an expert at getting an IV line into the smallest vein. After many months, when he reported that his hand had started shaking during this procedure, I told him it was time for a vacation. He took my advice, took some time off, and came back refreshed and strengthened — and with a steady hand.

CHAPTER 8

Putting It All Together

Below is a summary of how to put all this information into practice — practically.

Essentially, we are talking about two stress processes that need to be managed. Firstly, acute stress and anxiety that have actual symptoms of stress and panic and are clearly perceived and recognized. Secondly, chronic low-grade stress that often goes unnoticed but develops an array of dangerous effects that we have already mentioned. Acute stress situations need to be addressed by the various stress management techniques that have been described above. Chronic stress needs to be identified, and fundamental changes must be made to reduce the core issues and tone down the levels of stress.

You need to be very sensitive to low-grade sympathetic overdrive, such as feeling a slight tightness in your chest, a slight increase in your pulse or waking up in the morning feeling a bit anxious. Mindfulness and heightened awareness of stress is essential. The use of an app that measures heart rate variability can assist in increasing this awareness.

You simply need to attach a pulse monitor onto your chest and use a reliable app to measure your score. Keeping track of HRV is advantageous for the following two reasons. Firstly, it increases the awareness that circumstances cause the sympathetic stress system to become overactive. This will automatically help you avoid these situations. Secondly, you can start stress reduction intervention as soon as you detect a decrease in HRV, and thereafter you can monitor how effective it is in improving your stress response.

Now, once you have become more in touch with the symptoms of stress and the feelings associated with it, you need to identify the underlying cause of this stress. It is of limited value to just apply a stress-lowering technique without going through a quick check list that assists you in recognizing the source of the stress. Doing so can be compared to taking a Tylenol for pain as opposed to identifying the cause of the pain and treating the actual problem. Obviously, once you have identified the issue, it is in your best interest to deal with it and try and solve the problem.

So, here's what you should do.

1. Firstly, do a **quick review** of the list of the 7 Cs — causes of stress — to try and locate the trigger.

   - *Control:* Are there issues in your life that are beyond your control and causing the stress — be it financial, work related, family related or time related? It is important to locate the cause.

- *Completion:* Are there outstanding tasks that have yet to be completed? Procrastinating and putting things off tend to add stress to your life. Try making a to-do list and then tackle each task one by one. As you cross items off your list, it will take a weight off your shoulders. Make sure you set aside uninterrupted time to do this.

- *Cut out toxic exposure:* Is there someone bothering you or a situation that is stressful for you? Pinpoint the cause and write it down.

- *Concentration:* Are you unable to concentrate and complete various tasks thoroughly because you are multitasking? Write it down.

- *Conflict avoidance and resolution:* Is there an outstanding conflict that needs resolution or avoidance? Write it down.

- *Consistency — inside and outside:* Are you harboring any ongoing deceptions? Are there any inconsistencies in your life that you are concealing? Spell it out so that you can resolve it.

- *Creativity and purpose:* Are you waking up in the morning with an empty feeling, with no significant purpose or meaningful activity that needs to be done?

2. **Work out** which issues are relevant to you.

By thinking through the list of causes for stress you can increase your awareness of what is really worrying you. Discover which issue is playing on your mind and causing that tight chest that you could not pinpoint before. Once you recognize the cause, you are halfway there at reducing the stress.

3. **Develop a strategy** to overcome these issues.

You have now identified the source of your anxiety or stress. Now you have to strategize how to resolve it. The following game plans can be used:

- If possible, avoid the stressor or the cause of the stress, that in some cases could include a certain person or situation. Obviously there are people and circumstances that cannot be avoided, however, if they are not central to your life, try and stay away from them.

- Confront the cause of your stress and try and deal with it so that it becomes a workable situation again. As I have mentioned before, it is preferable to confront the person who is causing you stress and try and sort out the issues at hand. This would not work, however, if a confrontation would result in increased conflict and more damage.

An example of a positive situation could be if someone owes you money but keeps avoiding you, either because they do not want to pay you or are not financially able at the present time. The best solution would be for you to confront the person, discuss the situation and reach a settlement plan amicably. This could be in the form of payments or a settlement price that they can afford; either way, you will resolve the tension between you even if you come out with a little less money.

A negative situation occurs when you confront someone about an issue and no solution can be reached. An example of this could be someone who is very aggressive and is unable to see the other side of the picture and only perceives their side of the story. You may need to avoid this type of person and instead work on your own attitude, attaining peace of mind, even if it means losing out financially.

As a physician, I have had situations where people have been aggressive and tried to push for their needs without reason. I used to argue with them, and on occasion I had to ask a patient to leave the office. At the end of the day, it was not worth the battle and the added stress that accompanied it. I have learned to speak calmly and do what I can for this type of individual without compromising on any real medical risk, and in the end, the patient leaves my office peacefully.

COMPROMISING is of fundamental importance, as it results in a win-win situation. It is helpful if you realize that by compromising a LITTLE, you can prevent a LOT of extra stress and frustration. The excessive stress aroused when fighting for your perceived rights can lead to days of wasted energy trying to beat your opponent, and more often than not, leads to major legal costs in order to try and win. This cost may be more than the money that you stand to lose.

It is extremely beneficial to take on the attitude that you are not going to clash with your opponent, whether it is a business partner, husband, wife or any other challenger, even if they push for this. It is always good to take the peaceful approach and explain to the opposing party that you'd prefer to settle the issue in a FAIR way. Speak openly and try and work out the issue even if you lose out for the sake of peace. It is better to try and compromise so that both parties come out alright. Although there are times when the other party is too obstinate and won't seek a compromise in order to avoid conflict and extra costs, most often this is not the case, and you are quite likely to be successful.

4. You need to be resolute to make the necessary changes, even if it means making a major change in your life, in order to reduce your stress and give yourself a chance to improve your overall well-being. In situations where you have identified the cause of your stress as being a central part of your life and daily activity, and it is unavoidable, you have to assess the situation carefully and decide on the appropriate action that is required.

This may involve being courageous and taking a drastic step, such as changing jobs or confronting a relationship issue by way of a therapist. These changes should only be implemented after careful consideration and planning. For example, you should not give up your job, if you are the sole breadwinner and your family is dependent upon your monthly income, before finding another job. This entails submitting applications, going for interviews and signing on another position before making the move.

The same would apply to toxic relationships. You would initially investigate if there is a way to improve things, exhausting all avenues first. If, for example, your spouse is the problem, you may want to try all methods to resolve the difficulties before considering a separation. Remember that although the "grass looks greener on the other side," this is not always the case and is often an illusion. However, when all considerations have been carefully assessed, there are times when a move is essential. Remaining in a toxic situation can be too damaging, and a positive move may be necessary to improve the situation. Take the plunge — you only live once!

5. Remember: life should be lived in a tranquil, positive and comfortable mode. Every day must be filled with useful, creative and enjoyable activities.

You should work hard but maintain a balance between work and your home life. Your job should be a positive working experience accompanied by sufficient down time to relax and rejuvenate, especially after hours and on weekends. Creating warm, deep personal relationships with friends and family should be a priority, and using your smile muscles more than your frown muscles will benefit all those around you. When you feel things are going wrong, you need to address the situation; ignoring it and pushing it aside can develop toxic effects of stress that will ultimately take a toll on your health.

You need to be in touch with even subtle stress effects so that you can develop mindfulness and fine-tune a lifestyle that is conducive to good health and prosperity. This includes healthy nutrition, proper sleep habits and daily exercise.

Here are a couple of real-life examples of the destructive effects of unrecognized stress that I have managed in my medical practice.

There is a middle-aged woman with kidney disease that resulted from her diabetes, although she has been stable for years. Recently, her kidney function deteriorated for no apparent reason, albeit her blood pressure increased slightly. Together with her nephrologist, we completed a full blood work-up without finding the reason for her deterioration. When she returned for an appointment together with her husband, I took one look at her facial expressions and body language and realized that she was overly stressed. I immediately inquired as to her personal situation at home, only to be told that she was working too hard and was experiencing problems with her son. This in turn was having an effect on her sleep patterns. (A salivary cortisol test showed high cortisol levels). I told her that stress was the reason her blood pressure had increased, leading to excessive pressure on her small blood vessels in the kidneys and inflammation in her body. I also explained that the lack of vagal tone prevents the suppression of inflammation and damage from the immune response. I advised her to stop and reassess the situation and make several fundamental changes. After changing her work pace and finding solutions to the family problems, things settled down again and her medical condition stabilized.

Another patient — a 40-year-old male — presented with weakness, bloody diarrhea and abdominal pain. After a full workup with a gastroenterologist, he was diagnosed with Ulcerative Colitis, an autoimmune disease, whereby antibodies attack the intestine causing inflammation. He decided to treat the disease naturally with a strict diet. This treatment definitely improved the situation. Occasionally, he experienced some flare-ups and needed a course of steroids to calm down the inflammation, but all in all, he seemed to be managing nicely and keeping the disease under control. However, recently, he started losing weight, and the colitis flared up and nothing seemed to help quiet it down. I inquired about his lifestyle and discovered that beside the fact that he was enduring financial hardships, he was trying to complete a difficult degree at night whilst working full time during the day. He was extremely stressed, and I told him that he could not heal his body under such stressful conditions. I advised him to take a step back, review his life and make some important changes. Attempting to take on the extra degree was too taxing on his medical condition, and he needed help to realign his life and his career choice in order to start healing and coping with his situation. He obviously had an uncontrolled inflammatory cascade occurring in his body and no vagal tone to dampen this response.

There are more subtle examples whereby the causes of stress are not so obvious, but you have to nevertheless step back and review what is happening in your life in order to detect the source of stress.

Other classic examples may be in-laws who are due to arrive and stay in your home for two weeks, forgetting about a scheduled presentation at work, or certain people in your life who seem to make your blood pressure rise every time you meet them. Going through a divorce, moving to a new house, financial issues and medical concerns are among the top stress inducers that you can experience. Sometimes a medical problem can take a number of weeks before an answer is received, such as in the case where a dark mole is removed by a dermatologist, and the results of the biopsy are only available after a week. Although one may continue life as normal, subconsciously, the underlying stress is ever-present.

In all the above cases, the subconscious brain remembers the stress and ignites the stress response even if the conscious awareness has forgotten about the underlying cause. Therefore, it is important to go through the checklist that will link the stress with the subconscious cause in order to take preventative action.

Inertia

Having described the process to confront stress head on and deal with it, there will always be the aspect of inertia. This is the tendency to remain in your comfort zone and not want to step out and make any changes. As a physician, there are so many examples where I have tried to change people's habits or behavior, having expended an inordinate amount of time describing the major health benefits, and yet at each subsequent visit there is no change for the better.

An example of this is my patient whose main health problem is stress. He has already had a minor stroke even though most of his health profile is quite good, including cholesterol levels, glucose and other blood parameters. We focused on the changes that he had to make in order to reduce the stress burden in his life, but to date, he is still in the same situation. He would like to adjust his lifestyle and he understands the benefits, but he cannot get it together to make the drastically needed shifts that might save his life. He is too preoccupied with his problems and cannot pull himself together to bring about these changes.

Another example is the young couple who are in a financial mess. The wife is collapsing under pressure waiting for a job promise that is not materializing. Instead of lingering in limbo and waiting and hoping, they need to change direction to break out of their predicament and find a solution.

HOW TO BREAK THE INERTIA

You cannot break out of an impossible situation without taking time to deal with it. Even if you have taken the necessary steps to recognize the stress and identify the root causes, if you do not spend time planning a solution, then life's daily challenges will keep you too preoccupied to make any changes. This applies to any changes that you want to make in your life. You can be totally convinced that you need to lose weight and improve your health profile, but if you are too busy and don't take an active step forward, there is no way you will transform out of your old habits. Inertia and a so-called comfort zone will keep you rolling along in your usual routine, even if you are heading for disaster.

The message remains — change requires planning and focus. People who are successful in changing their habits are those who invest in the change. It is often uncomfortable and even frightening to make a serious move, but you need to be adaptable. In other words, if one option does not work out, be creative and look for an alternative. If the one job option does not look like it is going to materialize, look for an alternative immediately and always stay positive.

I would like to summarize our approach to change as follows:

RECOGNIZE	**Recognize** the symptoms of stress and don't ignore them.
DETECT	Search for and **detect** the root causes of the stress.
FORMULATE	Spend time **formulating** a plan of action to resolve the stress-causing problems.
CHANGE	Make the necessary **changes**.

STRESS DIARY

A stress diary may be very helpful to organize your thoughts and put the above principles into practice. By writing down your ideas and possible solutions, it makes you really think about your problems and face up to them. Often, seeing something in writing sets out the issues more clearly and enables you to formulate a plan to address and manage your stress mode. Filling out the diary on a weekly basis will give you an insight as to how you are coping and enable you to make the necessary adjustments as needed.

STRESS SYMPTOMS	CAUSE	MY REACTION
Example: 1. Cold sweaty hands	Angry Boss	Keep quiet
PLAN OF ACTION	*Work on responding confidently and firmly to his aggression.*	
2. Rapid breathing	Fear of going into elevators	Break into a cold sweat
PLAN OF ACTION	*Make sure to go in with other people at first, slowing building up your confidence to go in an elevator on your own.*	
3. Rapid pulse, feeling of fear and anxiety	Giving a public presentation	Feeling nervous and giving over an inarticulate speech
PLAN OF ACTION	*To work on your confidence and eloquence. Gain as much knowledge as you can about the topic you are speaking about, and practice giving it over without worrying about the reaction of your audience.*	

After filling out the stress diary for one week, you should analyze how you responded and then see what your plan of action should be. Resolve to make the appropriate changes to your response and try and implement these changes. If your boss loses his temper again, respond firmly to him and explain your actions. With a response plan in place, it will give you confidence to deal with stressful situations and not allow them to affect you physically or emotionally. If you feel your response was incorrect, reassess it and try again.

REPLACEMENT THERAPY

Those of us who have become stuck with certain unhealthy habits and find it impossible to change, may need to use replacement therapy.

For example: I have a patient who smokes and will not consider stopping despite the onset of early emphysema. I started him on a graded exercise program, increasing the intensity in stages, whilst at the same time, I advised him to continue smoking. As he became more fit and needed more lung capacity to increase the exercise, I started weaning him off the cigarettes slowly. His unhealthy smoking addiction was gradually being replaced by a healthy addiction to exercise and after some time, he succeeded in becoming smoke-free and a happier, healthier man.

The same principle can be applied to any addiction that is bad for you. Namely, first begin slowly with a healthy replacement and then reduce the addictive agent. This means that you do not tackle the addiction head on, but rather strengthen other areas until you have much less of a need for the addictive agent. The same idea can be applied to stressors in your life. Rather than trying to face certain stressors head on, you may need to spend time strengthening yourself and giving yourself recovery time in order to continue. Once you are in a stronger state of mind by applying the techniques that were discussed above, you can then face the stressful situation directly and make the appropriate changes.

My Take on Oxytocin

There is a school of thought that maintains that stress is not necessarily a bad thing, nor does it increase the risk for cardiovascular disease and other illnesses. In fact, they claim that there is evidence that if you have the correct attitude to a stressful situation, it may even be beneficial for you. If you do not perceive stress as a cause for concern, then that in itself lowers your risk. On the other hand, if you fear stress as a potential danger to your health, then your chances of becoming ill will increase.

There is a hormone in the brain called oxytocin that is released with stress. It counteracts the effects of cortisol and can reduce blood pressure and relax the arterial walls of blood vessels.

The positive effects of oxytocin are that it turns stress into something constructive. Instead of feeling cornered and threatened by stress, the idea is that we should use the situation to be proactive and grow from the experience by facing up to the challenge.

Not only is oxytocin associated with counteracting cortisol, it is also known as a social hormone, which is released during social and physical contact, such as hugging. It is also released during breast feeding, when temperatures are warmer, and even when we come into contact with certain smells and sounds.

By sharing your stress with someone close to you and by having social contact with other people, it can further enhance the positive effects of oxytocin. Enduring stress without support can have a negative effect on your health.

Try and put some thought into the situation at hand. Be resourceful — it can lead to personal growth and strength. Instead of panicking and feeling trapped, you can modulate your response and convert it to a positive experience. In order to do this, you need to be mindful and create a plan of action. Think of different ideas. If need be, seek professional help or assistance from support groups, friends or relatives. Exchange ideas and concerns. This will not only help strengthen you but will give you the courage and ability to tackle and rise above the stress.

This model appears to view stress and your response to it in a very chemical way. It is based on reducing the cortisol and increasing the oxytocin effect. These are physiological responses to stress, however, the real driver of how we manage stress is not our hormone balance but really the human spirit behind it all.

You can view your ambition, drive and reactions based on the release of hormones and neurotransmitters in the brain, but essentially, it is you, the individual, who will determine what you do and how you do it despite these hormones and chemicals.

You may have a sudden urge to do something out-of-the-ordinary that could have enjoyable short-term benefits but could cause disastrous long-term damage. You, the driver, can stand back and decide not to follow your impulsive urge, but to rather turn away from the desire and need for instant gratification. This ability to refrain from acting impulsively can give you a sense of great satisfaction that you managed to succeed.

In much the same way, acute stress will have different effects on your brain and body. However, it is not the chemicals that need to determine your response but rather your ability to choose your direction. At the end of the day, no matter what your chemicals are doing, you as a person can choose how you are going to react. Stay mindful and remember, the outcome is your choice – not chemical based.

Mindfulness definitely assists in overcoming the challenge. By standing back, viewing your options and being creative and brave, you can make clear-cut positive decisions in a stressful situation in the same way as you would fight a negative desire that could be detrimental to you.

In the 21st century we have discovered and made known to the world major risk factors for disease. We have moved from infections being the main cause of illnesses and death to heart attacks, strokes and cancer. Some of the known risk factors include poor nutrition, smoking, lack of exercise, excess alcohol, obesity and high blood pressure. Parameters in the blood that can be measured are high cholesterol, triglycerides and glucose.

The human genetic coding has been unraveled, and associations with many illnesses are being made. The management of genetic defects and gene expression is the focus of the medical world today and will provide exciting breakthroughs to many treatments in the coming years. However, changes in lifestyle, which includes the stresses of modern-day living, have an overriding influence on all of the above factors and have not been adequately addressed in the medical field.

Stress and life satisfaction impact the way we live in modern times. The overall significance on our health parameters is immense. There is a close correlation between stress and heart attacks, strokes and cancer incidences. The stress hormones also influence our metabolism, as well as most body functions, including the expression of our genes. It is possible to have a dangerous gene defect that could cause significant health problems, but that remains dormant without expressing itself. However, stress may cause this negative gene to become active and lead to health issues.

On the other hand, the vagus parasympathetic system promotes many protective effects on the body and prevents the onset of a variety of diseases. A greater emphasis amongst the amazing medical advances needs to be placed on improving our life satisfaction, decreasing our stress and moving into a tranquil, useful and constructive outlook. If we forget this aspect, we are likely to "miss the boat."

PART II

MAKING EVERY DAY COUNT

Now that we have learned and understood how to live a more tranquil and stress-free life, we need to master how to infuse value into our lives — thereby adding life to our years. This entails making positive strides towards attaining more meaning and purpose, lest we inflict a new stress upon ourselves by not having fulfilling goals.

There are a number of activities and feelings that have a different physiological effect on us, and this can be felt physically. As we discussed in the first section of the book, stress can cause tightness in our chest. However, when we feel relaxed, our breathing is totally subconscious and automatic, and is performed without any awareness or effort.

Other examples include the "feel good feeling" we experience when we have achieved something worthwhile through hard effort, or when we help or rescue someone. These positive feelings are actually healthy signs and mean that our body is doing physiologically well.

We now have evidence that contributing to others and feeling worthwhile and useful, as well as functioning in vagal tone, all have valuable medical benefits. Therefore, in this section of the book, we will investigate how to further enhance our lives, and in so doing, improve our overall health.

It is important to investigate how we use our time and how we can build useful valuable time in order to make a lasting difference to us and those around us, with the additional years of life we are given. Time is an important commodity that is valuable and irretrievable. It is worth learning how to best use and enjoy it to its fullest.

The same hour, day or year can be very different depending on how we use it. A good day, well spent, may be more useful and significant than a year that was wasted. Therefore, by using our time correctly, we can make life more worthwhile at any age or stage. We can learn how to accumulate thousands of days and not allow the years to fly past. We will discuss how time can be slowed down and how to effectively lengthen our days.

THE CONCEPT

Time can be stored and preserved in the same way flowing water can be dammed. By making each day full and significant, an entire life can be enriched. This time need never be lost but rather, it can be encapsulated into our lives so that our days and experiences are accumulated. As our days grow richer and fuller with a life so worthwhile, time is never lost.

The mechanism of how to encapsulate time and enrich life with each day will be discussed in this section of the book.

The alternative to this will be to watch time fly past, each year feeling shorter than the previous one. Ultimately, our age progresses rapidly and we become dismayed by how quickly the decades advance and disappear. We feel that the years are slipping away and life is becoming shorter and shorter.

There are many theories and ideas about mindfulness; how essential it is to live in the present and increase your awareness and consciousness. This is certainly the way to capture the moment. With this in mind, the fundamental question remains: What are we capturing? I have spent many years pondering the subject of what is a useful activity and what activities will remain with us and become eternal time, or time that lasts.

I have reached the conclusion that from all the activities we do, there are only two types that are everlasting:

— Firstly, those that help build us as a person, be it through education, character development and acquiring good human qualities.

— Secondly, activities that contribute to others, including all those things that improve life for other people. We will discuss these concepts in more depth in the next section.

Man is like a breath;
his days are like a passing shadow - Psalm 144:4

I would like to investigate a different approach, one that will prevent our future time from fading and flitting away like the past has done. This approach will make each day a permanent addition to our lives and not another day lost.

We will see how selecting certain activities in our day-to-day living can encapsulate that period of time and make it an everlasting part of our lives. We will learn what type of activities will last and why.

Finally, we will also learn how to maximize our efforts in performing activities in a way that enables them to remain with us, so that we can convert our normal days into important and everlasting periods of time. We do not need to live merely from one big event to the next with everything being lost in between, but rather will take advantage of all the time we are given to make an impact on our own lives and that of those around us. We must remain engaged in life at any age, making sure to live each day to its fullest. This will help us recognize that there is a lot more living to be done, especially as we get older.

AGES

If we only knew back then what we know today, we would surely have done things differently and better. When I think back to my youth, young adulthood, my 40s and my 50s, I conclude that I would have done a much better job if I would have had my present experience. Enriching our lives should start as soon as we can recognize the value of making a useful life.

There is no specific age when you should start focusing on the big picture and valuing life. Any age can be a time of awakening, but there are two periods that are crucial to catch in order to adjust your direction and gain the most momentum. The first is the late 30s, going into the 40s; at this age, we have usually established a direction in life, and it is a good time to make sure that we are on a good track. The second is the late 50s and 60s. Here we are usually more established and have to ensure a solid direction for the second half of life.

CHAPTER 9

Activities That Last

So, what converts an activity into an eternal event?

There are two essential ways to create an eternal event:

1.   **By building and developing yourself.** Building yourself can be achieved in two ways:
a)   By realizing and developing a strength or talent.
b)   By succeeding in overcoming a weakness.

The end result of both of these achievements will be that you become more accomplished, more experienced or more knowledgeable, and ultimately achieve an increase in personal stature. These activities are character builders and remain with us for life.

2.   **By contributing and giving of yourself to others in order to make a difference in their lives.** Contributing to others or society can make a lasting difference and will become an eternal event that lasts.

The following are examples of the above concept.

9.1 Growth

We were born with certain talents, skills and character traits. Genetic inheritance contributes a large part to this make-up. Life experience will then create an impact on the initial package that we have inherited. From the first breath of an infant's life, physical, emotional and experiential factors mold the individual. At any point in time, your physical, emotional and intellectual capacity will have evolved to a certain place. However, you do not have to be constrained by this evolution. You can choose to grow at any time in any area, be it emotional, physical, intellectual or spiritual.

Over time, you are usually able to recognize your strengths which may shine through in the social sphere — you are very comfortable with social interaction; in the practical sphere — you are technical, creative or physical; or in the intellectual, academic sphere. Your natural talent should be developed, as it enables you to feel a sense of self-recognition and self-satisfaction, and it contributes to the all-important development of self-esteem.

It is important to realize that growth in any way will involve effort and challenge. Therefore, even when talents and strengths come naturally, it is important to have the self-discipline to develop these talents to the full.

On the flip side of the coin, you need to apply yourself in areas in which you are naturally weak. You have to overcome limitations and succeed in changing. For example, you may be limited in your intellectual ability, but with effort and perseverance, you may pass an exam or learn a new skill. This achievement becomes part of you, and you will feel satisfaction from your effort and success. It will be regarded as a permanent growth point and a part of your real-time development. Or perhaps you are limited by a tendency to anger with minimal provocation. With persistent work and understanding of this weakness, you can reduce the angry outbursts and eventually eradicate it. Once you feel more in control of this personality trait and are acting with less anger, it becomes part of the new you and will become integrated in your character.

Another mechanism for real growth is by contributing to others. Human beings have a higher dimension. If we are stuck in material and physical needs and pleasures for ourselves, we may never recognize the feeling of fulfillment and satisfaction by helping others and giving rather than just taking. The ensuing satisfaction and good feelings you achieve comes from seeing others benefit as opposed to self-indulgence. This growth comes from overcoming selfish drives for the sake of others. All these challenges, when successfully achieved, lead to personal growth. A more rounded and developed person emerges. Stature is built, character and personality are developed, and a worthwhile product unfolds.

Therefore, the success in personal growth is to recognize your strengths and to use them to develop and mature. This growth can occur in your profession, which may be in the practical, social or intellectual sphere, as well as in the other dimensions of your life. It is also crucial to recognize your weaknesses and undertaking to transform them one area at a time. This can be done by means of improving a character trait or skill in which you are weak. The time spent on this type of self-development becomes a part of you and remains with you.

9.2 Contributing

Life isn't about getting and having it's about giving and being.

What is the difference between being a taker and a giver? Givers are the people we meet and we feel enriched by the experience.

Have you ever entertained guests at your house, received clients at your office or patients in your clinic and felt that you gained something? In other words, there is no sense of loss even if you spent time, money and effort on them. The reason for this is that the person who was in your presence was a giver — orientated towards contributing — someone more interested in giving than taking.

Some people prefer giving more than receiving. If you give to them, they need to pay back more than you gave. But why is this important? Giving is important because it expands the human spirit. Contributing enables you to feel richer and not poorer. As a doctor for many years, I can honestly say that helping and treating patients is the most enriching activity I've experienced. Saving a life, feeding the poor, supporting the sick or even just being a friend at a time of need are all activities that bestow high value to the contributor. We will expand on this fundamental principle further on in the book.

Sometimes, though, taking is in fact giving. For those who rarely feel the need to receive, or even go as far as to turn down a favor or gift, graciously accepting something can in fact be a form of giving to the person who feels the desire to give or show appreciation. When you give of yourself and you experience the appreciation and effect on the recipient, you feel the benefit, not the loss. There is something deep inside that feels this satisfaction, and this type of giving remains with you as a permanent time activity.

9.3 Creativity

Creativity is the act of turning new and imaginative ideas into something real. It is characterized by the ability to perceive the world in new ways, to find hidden patterns, to make connections between seemingly unrelated phenomena and to generate solutions.

Creativity involves two processes: thinking followed by producing. If you have ideas, but don't act on them, you are imaginative but not creative. The following two quotes further define what it means to create.

"Creativity is the process of bringing something new into being. Creativity requires passion and commitment. It brings to our awareness what was previously hidden and points to new life. The experience is one of heightened consciousness: ecstasy."

— Rollo May, The Courage to Create

"A product is creative when it is (a) novel and (b) appropriate. A novel product is original not predictable. The bigger the concept and the more the product stimulates further work and ideas, the more the product is creative."

— Sternberg & Lubart, Defying the Crowd

All these unique angles come from a spark of inspiration and involve transformation into reality.

Creativity is a distinctive contribution of our personality, intelligence and spirit. By being innovative, we develop a unique and permanent offering. We are leaving a part of us behind. This is a worthwhile activity, and we should all be involved in this somehow even if we are not "naturally" creative. By living our life in our unique fashion, we are expressing creativity. Creativity is not only reserved for artists, musicians, architects and designers, but is within every person's reach.

Each one of us is unique, with no two people identical in every way. Finding this uniqueness and expressing it is our creativity. By doing so, we are providing an exceptional aspect of the thing that we are engaged in. This uniqueness can be expressed in the work we do, the family we raise, the food we prepare and even the way we relate to others.

We can identify and develop the unique and strong areas of our personality and capabilities. Some of us are stronger socially, whether individually or in groups. Some are stronger in building, repairing and designing. Some are stronger in the intellectual arenas, such as science, medicine, or research. However, when we do things in our own original way, with our own distinctive touch, we can make a difference. We leave a mark.

Whether it is for our family, company, city or country, we can make an unprecedented and lasting contribution. By discovering who we are and investing that uniqueness in what we do, we can make a real difference. The size and scope of this difference is not important, as long as the investment is done in our own authentic way.

I often think back and wonder how differently I could have done certain things if given a second chance, with my present knowledge and experience. Imagine realizing in your 20s how important it is to get a deep understanding and knowledge of your area of study and work, rather than just learning enough to pass the tests. With this maturity comes the realization that it would have been far more beneficial to complete an assigned task to the best of your ability, rather than rushing through the job in order to get to a movie on time. I remember some of the interns that I worked with who understood and implemented this concept and were able to excel in their work and studies and achieve so much at a young age.

Then the 30s arrived: marriage and young children could have happened with a balance of quality time at home, rather than working day and night at the expense of the family.

The 40s are a time for building deep foundations. Intensifying your understanding of your occupation, building firm financial foundations and paying more attention to your health definitely becomes a priority at this point in your life. This would also be the time to invest in lifelong friendships and relationships.

The 50s become a crucial time to invest in your health and prevent the beginning of real changes of aging. Many individuals start looking for new people to meet and for new experiences, rather than deepening present relationships and strengthening various aspects in your life.

The 60s-plus years may become the beginning of old age and retirement instead of the beginning of a new and exciting opportunity to realize new talents, learn new skills and contribute to a fuller and more meaningful life.

9.4 Why They Stay

We have spoken about growth, contribution and creativity. These are activities that make a lasting impression. Any episode of personal growth becomes part of us and grows with us.

Education, experience, overcoming weaknesses, developing strong positive character traits — all these areas remain with us and form part of the building blocks that constitute our being. Time invested in personal growth is eternal and is never lost. Contributing is giving of ourselves. It involves assisting and improving the lives of others. It involves committing a part of ourselves, such as giving of our time, lending money or teaching a skill to help or save others.

All this will make a difference both to the recipient of our giving and to ourselves.

So, the question can be asked: Can we recognize value-driven people? The answer is, most definitely yes. I have seen thousands of patients over many, many years in clinical medical practice, and of course one recognizes quality people with higher values. An example of this type of person is my patient who is in serious medical danger herself, and yet she always inquires as to my well-being and wishes me only health and happiness. And then there are my colleagues who are so thorough and caring for their patients, despite being under extreme pressure and fatigue. They do not cut corners in any respect and work to achieve the best medical results.

We have also seen community leaders and world leaders who are extremely value driven. Their main priority is for the best of their people and they have the courage and wisdom to make profound decisions. They have no self-interest, need for power or fame. They are value-driven individuals.

The personal growth attained when giving becomes a part of our stature and is never lost. Time spent giving is eternal time!

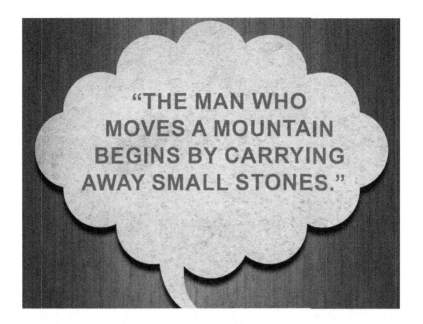

"THE MAN WHO MOVES A MOUNTAIN BEGINS BY CARRYING AWAY SMALL STONES."

Creativity lasts forever. By putting our uniqueness into our work, our family, friends, hobbies and interests, we are creating an everlasting heritage of ourselves, our personality, our talents and our character. Time used in creativity is everlasting time!

In other words, if we summarize who we are, we can say that we are a product of our personal development and growth. We are a summation of all the worthwhile things that we have achieved and done up until now. The truth is, though, that this growth and development should never stop. There is no retirement from working to prevent yourself from becoming passive and selfish. As we get older, we have more to give and share in wisdom and kindness and, in fact, we can even continue learning and being creative.

CHAPTER 10

Purpose

I find it very depressing to meet a teenager or young adult who has no motivation or meaning in life. There is no important mission to be achieved, and each new day is a burden, devoid of purpose. Drugs, alcohol, T.V. and social media become a way to occupy one's brain and time.

Dr. Viktor Frankl, M.D., Ph.D., an Austrian neurologist and psychiatrist, as well as a Holocaust survivor, describes meaning as "an essential drive in man." The lack of this basic drive is the cause of most psychological and existential problems. Meaning implies that you have a mission in life and that life has purpose and is not random. Meaning implies that there is a reason to live and that you must fulfill your purpose. It is vital to find this meaning and purpose, because this will give you direction in all of your activities.

Again, as described above, this purpose may be value driven such as improving yourself or helping others, and can be as large or small as you feel is necessary. In other words, some people are satisfied with their own personal growth and the health and wellness of their immediate family, whereas others may have the drive and ability to help communities and work on much larger projects.

When an individual's purpose is less value driven and more egotistical — where the main focus is on material wealth and power — there is a drive to achieve for self-gratification purposes only. This type of purpose may drive the individual but may not leave much of a legacy behind. It will not become part of an eternal quest, and the person may pass through this world without being remembered.

CHAPTER 11

Fulfilling Your Potential, Reaching Your Destiny

BIG things often have small beginnings

We have thus far discussed that you need to be motivated and determined to reach your goals. Furthermore, in order to achieve this, you have to be clear about what you want to accomplish.

We have described how you should spend time in activities that will build you or will contribute to others. Your activities need to make a difference.

Fulfilling Your Potential, Reaching Your Destiny

Each of us has been created with a unique set of talents and potential for growth. These talents are manifested in the presidents of large organizations, as well as the workers in fairly routine jobs. We all have to know where we are heading and aim to fulfill our own individual potential, whatever that may be.

It is essential to be satisfied with our abilities and not spend time pursuing levels that are far beyond our reach.

Two indicators help us direct our effort and time in order to gain real-time benefits.

Firstly, look at areas that come easy to us. We may have a natural talent. For example, we may have found carpentry to be enjoyable as a child and fixing things as an adult to be easy. We may have a social strength that makes working with people or groups flow naturally. We may have a scientific or artistic talent. These talents and strengths are usually recognizable during the development from childhood to adulthood. These strengths must be nurtured to their full potential in our home or work environment or in charitable causes or hobbies. Developing yourself through the enhancement of natural talents is a useful activity. This development becomes part of you and remains useful for the rest of your life.

The second sphere of development is to overcome areas of weakness, parts of your personality that are not natural strengths, or skills that do not come naturally. We may need to achieve this in order to arrive at a particular destination.

In our work, or at home, we may have to overcome a natural weakness in order to contribute to a final positive outcome. This is always a challenge and often very stressful, but success in this area is extremely fulfilling and very worthwhile.

An example would be a very competent computer programmer who needs to present an idea to a large group in his company. He may not be a fluent speaker and has a fear of public speaking. Facing the challenge and succeeding is a very valuable undertaking that will build character and stature. Often, outside help is needed to achieve the particular task.

A father who is excellent in a technical and practical way may spend his days repairing high power electricity lines, but he may be emotionally weak and unable to provide warmth or emotional support to his wife and children. The challenge of slowly showing more attention and love to the family and remembering to call home just to say "hi," to bring home flowers or play ball with his child will eventually become easier and will signify important growth. This work becomes useful, eternal time spent.

Another important area of challenge and personal growth is to refine your character and overcome bad personality and emotional traits. If you have a problem with anger, jealousy, stinginess or impatience, you must spend time overcoming these traits. For example, in the case of anger, growth can be measured each time you can count to 10 and avoid an outburst of anger or walk away from a meaningless conflict.

To overcome a stingy streak, you can force yourself to contribute on an ongoing basis to a worthy organization and slowly ingrain the characteristic of giving into your character.

Each success leads to another success and eventually you grow in your personal development. This effort is a worthwhile time activity and leads to the accumulation of eternal time.

CHAPTER 12

Building — Seeing the Big Picture

Life is filled with choices. When we make a decision to do one thing, it is often at the expense of something else. A classic choice is to decide to become financially secure so that you can retire and enjoy your retirement. You compromise on many important activities and events in order to accomplish this long-term goal; you work long hours, nights and weekends. You decide to give up the family vacation so that you can continue saving. You come late for important family functions. This drive can continue until you arrive at the very unfortunate situation that a friend recently told me about.

He is close to 50 and has more money than he can spend for the rest of his life. He is cutting back on his work to spend more time with his two sons. One is eighteen and going off to college but wants to spend some time in the East before entering college. He has so far refused all attempts at spending time with his father who is almost a stranger to him. The younger son of twelve has multiple emotional problems and has effectively grown up without a father. Has the financial security been worth the disastrous effects on his relationships with his children?

How often do we pursue friendships with powerful or influential people in the hope that we will gain from these contacts? We are frequently disappointed when these relationships end abruptly and do not lead to anything real or sustainable, despite the major investment of our time.

This investment of time has been at the expense of real, deep, life-long friendships that could have been cultivated with real people. The people who make up your life, like the man who fixes your car or your child's teacher, the man at the local store or the person you pray next to at your place of worship, these are all real people that can become real friends. Friends you can care for and who can care for you. By pursuing these friendships, you can build a wide circle of real friends who will always be there for you and will fill your life with a deep sense of caring.

Therefore, in making choices of how to invest time and with whom to cultivate relationships, we should look at the big picture. It is always good to start at home and make sure to invest in our closest relationships there. This is building with gold. Then invest with the people that make up the mosaic of our lives so that we build a wider circle of warmth and friendship. We should avoid the temptation to follow empty pursuits and worthless friendships because they appear to be sparkling and attractive from the outside.

I have a patient, Sara, who has multiple sclerosis. When she comes for her doctor's visit and I inquire how she is doing, she says, "Fine, there is nothing wrong with me." She is in her 70s and has significant disability, but she decided that MS is not going to hold her back, and she is going to live each day to the fullest. She feels blessed with what she has and does not allow her illness to interfere with her. She has overcome her disability and grows with each day.

Mindfulness

Now that we understand the importance of selecting value-type activities in our life, we need to recognize and place our focus on these specific activities whilst doing them. We may be involved in important valuable activities each day but are not appreciating or even noticing that this is happening. We can be with our kids and not realize they are with us, or we may take a partner or friend out to dinner and spend the time on our cell phones. We eat most of our meals without tasting the flavors, and travel through the countryside thinking about the office. In fact, we are missing a lot of life by not being in the moment.

Modern technology and the concept of instant gratification has helped create a generation of people with minimal concentration capacity. We need to work hard on spending small pieces of time concentrating on one subject and maintaining awareness of what we are doing. This will help us stay in touch with the experience, in order for it to have a lasting effect on us.

Most of us have a short concentration span and we may be involved momentarily in a task and then fade into a dream-like state or revert to other worries and thoughts. To remain in the moment and really live the experience is a skill and takes practice. You need to keep shifting yourself back to reality and seize the moment. Sustaining concentration levels is tough and requires ongoing work. Our minds wander continuously, and it is hard to stay focused on a particular subject for too long. The phenomenon of ADD and ADHD is so prevalent today that one of my most frequent prescriptions is for stimulants to help keep the brain focused and on track.

So how do we keep on track? We need to be AWARE of what we are doing and make a conscious effort to concentrate on the now and stay in the now. We need to notice what is happening and appreciate it. APPRECIATION is the name of the game.

Try waking up and noticing the view or the beautiful day outside, listening to the person you are talking to and tasting and appreciating the food you are eating. Being mindful is being in the moment. It is important to absorb meaningful things, to be grateful for them and make them a part of your memories. Our brains only remember things that we expend conscious energy on.

You must recognize the activity you're involved in and its importance, and then begin. You should even say to yourself that you are now beginning a value activity, and then mention the activity. Once you have started, if other thoughts and concerns creep into your mind, drive them out. If you are with somebody, ignore the messages on your mobile and look at your partner. Work on listening. Listening to a person is one of the most difficult activities because we have a need to spill out our own ideas or opinions. However, it is one of the most useful skills in life. People love a person who pays attention and hears what they have to say. I have a good friend who does not have a college degree in psychology or social work, and yet because she listens and cares for others, all types of people seek her advice and attention.

We need to use all our senses and appreciate what is happening. Mindfulness allows an event to make a difference and to have an effect on us. It will make the time spent on the activity become valuable and eternal. This time will remain with us. Doing things, even important things, in a semi-conscious way will not have any long-term effect on our lives — it is essentially time lost.

Another aspect of mindfulness is to recognize the positive aspect in what is happening. We may have much more than we recognize, without even knowing it. We can become aware of a pleasant day, tasty food, the absence of conflict, enough money to get through the month. These small gifts will help add to a positive feeling. The antithesis will be to sink into negative mode. We may have a headache, some joint pains or there may be blasting heat outside. Instead of concentrating on the positive, we get caught up with feeling sorry for ourselves and lose sight of the good things.

I have patients who have real reasons to complain, and yet they emphasize their good fortune of being alive and having friends and good people around them. If we concentrate on the good and change our mindset and attitude to reflect these intentions, then we can overcome many obstacles and negative influences in our lives and enjoy and focus on the positive, happy aspects.

A classic example of this was described by the famous psychologist Viktor Frankl, mentioned above, who lived through the concentration camps in Europe. Through the dread and misery of the camp, he noticed and watched a small tree from his barracks changing through the different seasons. He first saw the tree blossoming in spring, followed by the growth of leaves in summer and eventually the change of color and the falling leaves in autumn. He enjoyed those moments of freshness and newness, and this enabled him to maintain his sanity during those dreadful years.

We must focus and be mindful of the good while we have the chance, and by doing so, we may come to recognize that we have much more to be grateful for than we think.

CHAPTER 13

Putting It into Practice

We have discussed how important it is to infuse value activities into our day. We will now look at ways to practically implement this into our lives.

Selecting your Priorities

With a new understanding of what activities are going to build your life and remain with you, it is now important to make this process practical.

A life plan requires careful preparation in the same manner as instituting a new, healthy eating program requires planning. If you decide to begin an eating plan but healthy food is not available at home or at work, you will revert back to bad eating habits because you will be hungry and will eat whatever is easily accessible.

In a similar fashion, you need to spend time making a list of enduring events to select from each day. If you have a choice of quality activities, you can easily select a few for that day, and you will be prepared to act on them.

Putting It into Practice

An example of a list may include the following:

- Calling a friend who would appreciate a call
- Meeting a friend for coffee to build a relationship
- Spending quality time with a child

- Starting piano lessons again
- Completing the book you were writing
- Taking a course to enhance your career

- Calling on a neighbor who lives alone
- Working in a local soup kitchen
- Connecting with siblings
- Spending time with parents
- Going on a nature hike to appreciate the beauty
- Spending 15 minutes a day contemplating and appreciating the gifts and blessings you have been given

Plan your day – 5 minute planner

Spend a few minutes at night to select which activities from your list you want to do the following day. Choosing should not take more than five minutes. These are the activities that you are going to do with the awareness that they are important events and will contribute to making your day count. Make sure that you make time for these memorable activities during the day, so that you will feel that you have accomplished something meaningful and valuable.

You may prefer to do a weekly planner of quality events. On Saturday night or Sunday, plug in quality activities for the week, so that you have specific time periods assigned to take care of these tasks that would add meaning and depth to your life. This will ensure that one week does not roll into another with mundane routine and boredom. Instead, memories are created and, with them, a sense of anticipation for new activities in the upcoming week.

Sensitize your action — 30 second preparation

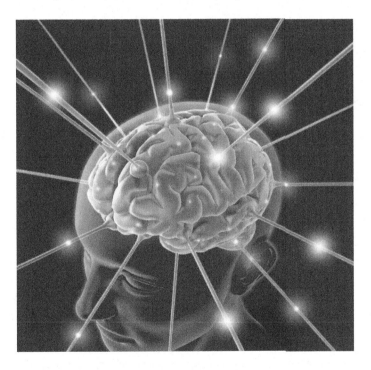

It is essential to ask the question: Why is this important *before* starting the activity?

Say to yourself, I am now starting a valuable event, and ask why it is significant. This practice will focus your attention on the activity and infuse quality in the activity that may otherwise have been done in a routine way without recognizing its value.

Example:

Activity: Quality time with Jay
WHY: To build a solid, trusting and deep relationship with my son

Activity: Work on writing a book
WHY: To express my unique idea of living life and to share it with others

Review the day — 5-minute backup

At the end of the day, or even before going to sleep at night, review the day. Consider the benefit of your valuable actions for the day and write them down in a journal.

For example: Think about the time spent with your son — How important was it? How can you make it even more valuable next time? Or, review the benefit you achieved by working on writing your book.

By reviewing these activities and saving the list, the activities become a part of you and are never lost. They become eternal events that fill your life, rather than being transient activities that go unnoticed and are lost forever.

Valuable activities that you take part in that are not from your list can also be saved by using the same method. There are numerous unplanned experiences that occur through a day that can be converted into a valuable event.

Example 1:

You may be starting an interaction with an employee or client or patient. You recognize that this can be a valuable event, so press the mental value event button and do your 30-second sensitizer.

Ask WHY this is important. In this case, the reason is to improve the position of the other party and to encourage him. Use your ability to make the meeting pleasant and helpful for the other party so that you can contribute something real and useful to them. This can be saved as a growing and useful experience for you.

Example 2:

You are going to meet a friend who has been calling you for weeks to make this arrangement.

Before meeting, do your 30-second sensitizer.

Put the WHY into the event. Your friend obviously needs this meeting; you will spend the time listening to your friend, assess what he or she may need and attempt to help. In this way, your friend will benefit from your attention, and you will gain a purposeful interaction that will be saved.

Now in theory this may sound nice and pretty simple to do, but who in the world can realistically put this together and put it into practice? It is true that it is not the natural way of doing things, and in fact, it is not simple to implement, but if you think about it, it is really not that complicated either. It might take a little practice on your part, but eventually it will start coming naturally to you, and you will get used to functioning like this, much the same way that you can become accustomed to buying healthy food and living a healthy lifestyle.

Try this now: Focus on the value of what you are doing by reading this book. You are learning a new skill that could enhance and change your quality of life in a dramatic way. The focus is on what is good and valuable to you. You will need to read this book again and try and implement a few of the practical ideas. Keep coming back to the exercises until it becomes part of your routine. Frequently, we start a process and then stop and get distracted or bored. Repetition of these exercises is good until you are really sensitized to making each day meaningful and inclusive of some special activities.

In life, there are choices. I can choose to start my day with the attitude of getting through the chaotic morning and pushing towards my break time as soon as possible, or I can focus on helping people, finding solutions for them and gain fulfillment and satisfaction from a meaningful, productive morning.

CHAPTER 14

Conclusion

This book has two aspects to it that can change your life. Firstly, you need to know how to select a few activities that are important to you and will remain and become part of your ongoing life. These activities will involve either personal growth or giving to others, and that will help mold who you are.

Secondly, you have to become more aware of what you are doing whilst partaking in important things. Recognize that you are doing something valuable and at the same time, be mindful of what you are doing. Some examples of this are hearing a spectacular lecture that can totally change your life, or spending an amazing time with someone important to you. These activities will not make a lasting impression on you unless you are aware of their importance before the event and evaluate them afterwards. In other words, you need to change from functioning in automatic mode to increased awareness of being in the present and focusing on the event at hand. In this way, the experience will remain with you and become integrated into your life.

Conclusion

Remember, we only live once. Don't let opportunities slip through your fingers. If you see a chance to patch up an old conflict, speak to a neighbor who always looks like they want to speak to you, apply for a new job you have wanted for a while, or sign up for a course you have been dreaming of, THEN DO IT! You will be amazed at how many channels will open up for you, and how one thing can lead to another. In this way, the richness of life will expand and bubble over.

In conclusion, you can make every day count. These days will contribute to building your life and will not be lost. You will have the opportunity to accumulate great personal growth with these eternal events, and this will be your heritage.

Instead of working your whole life in order to retire so that you can slow down and not do much, it is better to put this new model of life into place to prevent you from retiring and instead start up a new, exciting direction in life, with a new set of goals to achieve. In fact, leading a sedentary lifestyle speeds up aging.

Spend your working life in a balanced way, ensuring that you incorporate meaningful and important events in between your work and leisure time — thereby building who you are. Make your work purposeful so that you achieve a feeling of satisfaction for a job well done. When you retire, try to remain meaningfully busy. Although this means scaling down the work and converting to a slower mode of activity, it also means having more time for extra fulfilling things that fill and enrich your days. It is important to become involved in charity groups, starting a new career or trying new hobbies. Make sure you invest time and energy into valuable relationships in your life.

Do not look ahead and see how few years there are remaining — it could pull you down and stop you from enjoying your retirement. Instead, you need to take each day as it comes and make sure that you infuse usefulness and meaning into every day, making each day count.

At any age or stage of your life, you will see that each and every day presents an eternal opportunity for a lasting experience, providing you with years full of literally hundreds of meaningful days and events. This practice makes your days long and worth living and adds LIFE to your YEARS.

INDEX:

GLOSSARY OF TERMS:

Adaptogen: A natural substance considered to help the body adapt to stress and to exert a normalizing effect upon bodily processes.

Arrhythmia: A heartbeat that is irregular or an abnormal rhythm.

Colitis: Inflammation of the lining of the colon.

Cortisol: Hormone released by the adrenal cortex.

Endorphins: Hormones secreted within the brain and the nervous system that have a number of physiological functions.

Gamma Aminobutyric Acid (GABA): An amino acid that inhibits the transmission of nerve impulses in the nervous system.

Gene Expression: The process by which the instructions in our DNA are converted into a functional product, such as a protein.

Glycemic Index: A system that ranks food on a scale of 1 to 100 based on their effect on our blood sugar levels.

Heart Rate Variability (HRV): It is a measure that indicates how much variation there is in your heartbeats within a specific timeframe.

HPA Axis: Adrenaline is delivered into your neurobiological system by what is known as the hypothalamic-pituitary-adrenal axis, or the HPA axis. The HPA axis is named after three components: the hypothalamus, the pituitary gland, and the adrenal glands.

Insomnia: Inability to sleep.

Mindfulness: A mental state achieved by focusing one's awareness on the present moment.

Parasympathetic Nervous System: Known as the rest-and-digest system, it is responsible for conserving energy as it slows the heart rate and increases intestinal and gland activity.

7C System: The method used to determine your root cause of stress.

Sympathetic Nervous System: Known as the fight-or-flight system, it is the part of the nervous system that serves to accelerate the heart rate, constrict blood vessels, and raise blood pressure.

Sinoatrial Node: A small body of specialized muscle tissue in the wall of the right atrium of the heart that acts as a pacemaker by producing a contractile signal at regular intervals.

Vagus Nerve: Each of the tenth pair of cranial nerves, supplying the heart, lungs, upper digestive tract, and other organs of the chest and abdomen.

Vagal Tone: Vagal tone refers to activity of the vagus nerve, a fundamental component of the parasympathetic nervous system.

Made in the USA
Middletown, DE
20 May 2021